British Columbia

ROSEMARY NEERING

Whitecap Books

Vancouver / Toronto

The information in this book is true and complete to the best of our
knowledge. All recommendations are made without guarantee on the part
of the author or Whitecap Books Ltd. The author and publisher disclaim
any liability in connection with the use of this information. For additional
information please contact Whitecap Books Ltd., 1086 West Third Street,
North Vancouver, B.C., V7P 3J6.

Text by Rosemary Neering
Edited by Elaine Jones
Cover design by Warren Clark
Interior design by Margaret Ng
Cover photograph by Ron Watts / First Light
Typeset by CompuType

Printed and bound in Canada by D.W. Friesen and Sons Ltd.,
Altona, Manitoba

Canadian Cataloguing in Publication Data

Neering, Rosemary, 1945-
  British Columbia

  ISBN 1-55110-165-3
  1. British Columbia—Pictorial works. I. Title.
FC3812.N44 1994   917.1'0022'2   C94-910017-X
F1087.8.N44 1994

Contents

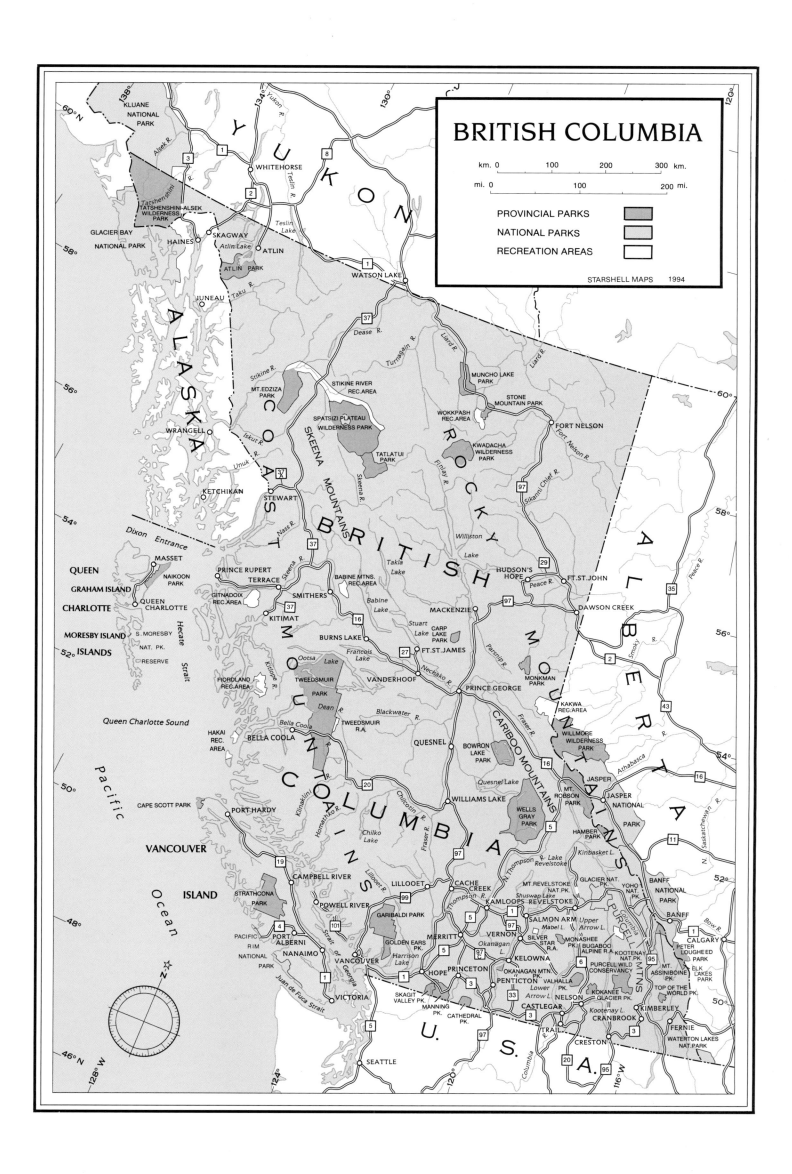

BRITISH COLUMBIA

km. 0   100   200   300 km.

mi. 0   100   200 mi.

PROVINCIAL PARKS

NATIONAL PARKS

RECREATION AREAS

STARSHELL MAPS   1994

Introduction

Pity the early explorer, sent from Europe or eastern Canada to map the wilderness of what is now British Columbia.

After months on the ocean, the seafarer finally approached the north Pacific coast. Land at last—but what land it was! Mountains rose sheer from the water, and evergreens mantled both slope and shore. The jagged coastline was deceiving, testing the navigator's every skill. After a season spent challenging the deep and silent inlets, bedevilled by fog and rain, eighteenth-century seamen fled happily back to the South Pacific islands to spend the winter.

The explorer by land crossed the wide expanse of forest and prairie, following crude maps or rumours that the Pacific Ocean was not far away. Then, thinking himself in reach of his goal, he saw ahead the formidable Rocky Mountains, echoed to the west by chain after chain of peaks whose existence he had barely suspected, rivers that flowed north but ended far to the south, and rapids and canyons that dismayed even the vaunted voyageurs.

A good thing, then, for Europe that British Columbia lay on the western edge of the continent. Had Europeans first encountered this land rather than the east coast of Canada, they might have retreated rapidly and stayed at home for centuries.

Modern travellers, armed with maps and prepared by photographs, have it easier. Yet even now it is difficult to get a sense of the overall topography of British Columbia's rugged mountain chains, long and narrow lakes, sparse green lowlands, sunburned plateau, winding rivers, and vast stretches of forest.

Billions of years ago, slow but violent geological forces glued much of this land to the continental spine. Millions of years ago, the earth's crust ruptured and twisted and volcanoes erupted, spilling lava across the land. Thousands of years ago, glacial ice advanced and retreated, scouring, sculpting, and leaving debris behind.

The geological upheaval is evident in the landscape. Seventy-five per cent of British Columbia lies more than a thousand metres above sea level. The province contains some ten major mountain systems, comprised of more than thirty ranges. A broad plateau, traced by ancient lava flows and deeply incised by erosion, covers more than one-fifth of B.C. A half dozen great river systems lie all or partly within the region.

The jumbled landscape has greatly influenced human habitation. Most theories suggest native peoples moved through British Columbia along valleys and rivers opened as the glacial ice receded thousands of years ago. The wealthiest native societies developed along or near the coast, where magnificent cedar forests provided raw materials for housing, canoes, tools, clothing, and artistic creations, and salmon and other sea creatures were the basis of a rich diet. In the interior, where resources were less plentiful and the climate harsher, native nations moved with the seasons, reaping the resources that the land, rivers, and lakes offered.

Like those early native societies, the first non-natives to reach British Columbia went where resources were most plentiful. Fur traders built posts in the interior and sent their ships along the coast. Prospectors tapped into rich veins of gold, silver, copper, and lead; mining camps and service towns sprang up wherever there was money to be made. Loggers invaded the forests of coast and interior; many of today's cities and towns began as logging camps. Farmers established cattle ranches in the Cariboo, dairy and mixed farms in the Fraser Valley and on Vancouver Island, orchards in the Okanagan, wheat fields in the Peace River Valley.

In the late nineteenth and in the twentieth century, railroads and highways transformed the province. Those transportation systems followed the natural contours of valley and river; cities and towns grew rapidly along road and rail.

Though the changes were great, the mountainous, harsh,

and beautiful topography still held sway: British Columbia today remains lightly populated. Two and a half times the size of Japan, four times larger than the United Kingdom, bigger than California, Washington, and Oregon combined, the province contains just over 3 million people, a little more than three to each of its almost 1 million square kilometres.

More than two-thirds live in the southwest corner of the province: in Greater Vancouver at the mouth of the Fraser River, in the Fraser Valley, or on the southeastern coast of Vancouver Island, where the terrain is manageable and the climate moderate. Most of the rest are clustered along lake and river valleys in the interior.

A hardy few still live the pioneer legends of a frontier province, thriving in the wilderness that so challenged the early explorers of British Columbia.

Opposite: *Totem poles stand in front of seven tribal houses at 'Ksan, a re-created Gitksan tribal village near Hazelton. Visitors can see Gitksan artists and dancers and hear the stories of the treasure room and exhibition centre, the carving shed, the studio, the 'Ksan shop, the Fireweed House, the Wolf or Feast House, and the Frog House of the Stone Age.*

Victoria, Vancouver Island, and the Gulf Islands

On the west coast of Vancouver Island, wind-driven waves crash onto rocky headlands, and salt spray sifts over the cedars and hemlock at the water's edge. The steep slopes of the mountains that form the island's spine rise sharply from the ragged coastline, and rain slashes down from clouds driven upwards over the mountains.

On the southeast tip of the island, civil servants sip caffe latte in Victoria's sunshine, and plan their weekend tennis games. Not far away, joggers trot along the waterfront, past seniors who lead small dogs below the craggy Garry oaks and between the daffodils.

Wild and tamed, fierce and gentle, extreme and moderate: the contrast has always defined Vancouver Island. Glaciers dragged their sharp and icy fingers over the west coast, creating a serrated landscape. They dealt more gently with the southern tip and southeast coast, leaving behind rocky meadows and a narrow coastal plain that extends halfway up the island. Offshore, dry because they lie in the rain shadow of the mountains, are the gentle hills of the Gulf Islands.

In the early days, the wilder, wetter coasts favoured human habitation. The native peoples of the west coast and north island developed some of North America's richest societies, bolstered by the resources of salmon stream, ocean, and rainforest. Early explorers also built their temporary posts on the west coast, where they could trade with the native peoples.

But when non-natives, not so firmly tied to the resources on their doorsteps, made permanent homes on the island, they settled on the sheltered southern tip. The Hudson's Bay Company established Fort Victoria; the wave of prospectors who arrived during the Cariboo Gold Rush from 1858 to 1870 ensured that the fur-trading fort would grow to a thriving town. Victoria became the capital of British Columbia and the administrative centre of the island. Miners, loggers, and farmers took advantage of the resources of the east coast to establish communities such as Nanaimo, Courtenay, and Campbell River. Though the native peoples continued to live along all the island's coasts, the focus had shifted from the wild west coast to the quieter east.

The pattern established in the nineteenth century continues. More than half the region's 600,000 people live in Greater Victoria, on a small fraction of Vancouver Island's 32,261 square kilometres. Less than 3 per cent of the population live on the north half of the island, an equally small number on the west coast.

But the people who crowd the urban areas are increasingly interested in the wilder regions. Over the last decade, more and more islanders and outsiders have rediscovered the west coast: Pacific Rim National Park attracts hundreds of thousands of visitors every year, and environmentalists are staging fierce battles to save what remains of Vancouver Island's majestic rainforest. For them, as for others, the enduring contrast between wild and tamed is the essence of the island.

Opposite: *The Sunken Garden, at Butchart Gardens near Victoria, occupies what used to be an unprepossessing limestone quarry pit. Jenny Butchart, wife of the quarry owner, had tonnes of soil brought to this site by horse and cart, to create the first showpiece in what is today ten hectares of gardens containing more than a million plants.*

Above: This carriage-for-hire in downtown Victoria recalls an earlier era, when horse-drawn transportation took Victorians about their daily round of work and pleasure. Horse-drawn hacks lined up along the main streets, their drivers in the nearby pubs, waiting for fares. Everyone who was anyone had horses and carriages, barns, grooms, and coachmen.

Opposite: A sidewalk cafe outside a pub-restaurant on Victoria's Store Street is part of the restoration and beautification of the city's Old Town. Left to decay until the late 1960s, this earliest part of Victoria now gleams with bright paint, red brick, and sculpted stone.

Previous pages: Some of Victoria's famed hanging baskets—twenty-six plants to each—provide a foreground for the Empress Hotel. Built in 1907 as part of the Canadian Pacific hotel chain, the chateau-styled Empress is supported by pilings on what used to be a tidal mudflat. The Empress has been expanded and refurbished several times.

Victoria, 1876

All was, supposedly, joyous celebration when the Marquess of Dufferin, governor-general of Canada, visited Victoria in August of 1876. His procession passed through a number of welcoming arches, such as this one, and balls, dinners, garden parties, and regattas were held in the governor-general's honour.

But just around the corner from this arch was another, under which Lord Dufferin refused to pass. "Carnarvon Terms or Separation!" it proclaimed, expressing the dissatisfaction many Victorians felt with the Canadian union they had entered into five years earlier. In 1878, members of the provincial legislature voted to ask Queen Victoria to let B.C. leave Canada.

The anger stemmed from broken promises, among them a pledge that a railway would span the country within ten years of British Columbia's entering Confederation in 1871. Little had been done on the project, and the Canadian government made several attempts to persuade British Columbia that no railway was needed after all. The railway was finally completed to the coast in 1885, and B.C. remained part of Canada. But it was a bad beginning: ever since then, British Columbians have viewed the federal government with some mistrust. (BCARS 8009)

Opposite: *Coal baron, railway magnate, and entrepreneur Robert Dunsmuir built Craigdarroch Castle in 1889 as a visible symbol of his wealth and prestige. Dunsmuir died before it could be completed. His widow, Joan, increasingly reclusive, lived in the mansion until her death in 1908. The castle became, successively, a hospital, a college, school board offices, and a music conservatory. It is now a restored period piece open to the public.*

Above: The formal flowerbeds and naturalized west coast plants of Beacon Hill Park in Victoria attract residents and visitors alike to this seventy-four-hectare retreat near downtown. Much of the park, from the waterfront cliffs to the meadows where blue native camas bloom and Garry oaks grow, was reserved as parkland almost 150 years ago.

Opposite: The statue of Queen Victoria is an apt companion for B.C.'s Parliament Buildings on Victoria's Inner Harbour. Though the buildings did not open until 1898, they were first illuminated in 1897, to celebrate the queen's diamond jubilee. Thousands gathered at the buildings in 1901, to mourn her death.

Overleaf: Sailboats wait for the start of the Swiftsure Yacht Classic, held each May. The first Swiftsure was held in 1930; now, some 350 boats race annually from Victoria to a mark ship anchored off Cape Beale near Bamfield, and back. Swiftsure weekend is a busy one in Victoria as race crews and rubberneckers crowd the Inner Harbour, where many of the boats tie up before the race.

Campbell River, 1926

From the day the native peoples of Vancouver Island built their first big house and carved their first totem pole, the tall, straight trees of the island have been central to its economy. By the time these loggers posed in front of a steam-powered, donkey-engined log skidder near Campbell River in 1926, there were probably several hundred logging camps on Vancouver Island, from tiny floating gyppos to large camps with post offices, schools, hospitals, hotels, and telegraph offices. By 1929, there were 250 sawmills on Vancouver Island and the Lower Mainland combined, and the first pulp mills were operating on the island. Many an island town was, at birth, a logging camp.

In the hundred and fifty years of commercial logging on the island, technology has dictated many changes. Early loggers worked with hand saws and horses; by the turn of the century, steam powered some logging machinery, and oxen dragged logs from the forest to the water. Diesel power and, especially, logging railroads picked up the pace of logging. Since then, the building of logging roads and the introduction of chainsaws and other technology have seen ever more trees cut by ever fewer people. Logging now is at the centre of a controversy that sees environmentalists and the logging industry battle over Vancouver Island's remaining forests. (BCARS 67783)

Opposite: *Saltspring Island is, at 180 square kilometres, the largest of the Gulf Islands that lie in the Strait of Georgia, between Vancouver Island and the mainland. Named for its fourteen salt springs, this island is changing slowly from a sylvan retreat known for its lamb and other farm products to a more crowded haven for disillusioned urbanites.*

Above: Barkley Sound, more than six hundred square kilometres of Pacific beauty southeast of Ucluelet, bears the name of Captain Charles Barkley and his wife, Frances, who anchored here while seeking sea otter skins in 1787. In its centre are the Broken Group Islands, part of Pacific Rim National Park and a favourite destination for canoeists and kayakers.

Opposite: Fishing and pleasure boats tie up at Tofino, on Vancouver Island's west coast near Pacific Rim National Park. The town of eleven hundred, long home to the native Nuu-chah-nulth, has been primarily a fishing village. Now it is also a destination for tourists.

Above: Ferns and seedlings on the forest floor at Cathedral Grove. Located between Parksville and Port Alberni, this is one of the few patches of readily accessible old-growth rainforest on the island. Giant Douglas fir, western hemlock, and western red cedar give a glimpse of the way the island's forests looked before logging.

Opposite: Nine thousand people come every year from around the world to hike the West Coast Trail, seventy-seven kilometres of beach and forest walking along the route of an old telegraph and life-saving trail between Port Renfrew and Bamfield. The trip takes five to seven days; it has become so popular that hikers must have permits.

Above: The burial ground at Alert Bay, on Cormorant Island, is on the land of the Nimpkish band of the Kwakwaka'wakw people. The memorial poles in the burial ground and the repatriated potlatch collection in the nearby U'Mista Cultural Centre testify to the artistic and traditional power of the Kwakwaka'wakw culture.

Opposite: Long Beach reaches thirty kilometres along the west coast, half long stretches of sandy beach, half rocky coves and headlands. No land intervenes between the beach, part of Pacific Rim National Park, and Japan, seven thousand kilometres westward across the ocean.

Overleaf: The forested shores of Clayoquot Sound, on Vancouver Island's west coast near Tofino, have been at the centre of a bitter battle between environmentalists, from British Columbia and around the world, who want to see its old-growth forest preserved, and forest companies, that want to log a large part of it.

Vancouver and the Fraser Valley

The potential of the Fraser Valley was not particularly evident to those who arrived here in the eighteenth and much of the nineteenth centuries. Captain George Vancouver's crew, charting the region in 1792, dismissed the river as navigable only by canoes. Simon Fraser traced the Fraser to its mouth in 1806 and declared that its canyons and rapids made it useless as a trade route.

When gold rushers crowded upriver in 1858, they saw the river only as a route to the riches of the interior. Would-be farmers who arrived in the northwest in mid-century preferred the meadows of southeast Vancouver Island or the open plateau of the Cariboo to the marshy, muddy, mosquito-ridden land along the Fraser.

Yet today more than half of British Columbia's population lives within a hundred kilometres of the river's mouth. Vancouver is Canada's third-largest city, and the cities and towns of the Fraser Valley are growing so fast they seem transformed almost overnight. Clearly, the twentieth century has discovered something the previous centuries did not.

The basic topography of the region remains the same. In the twelve hundred kilometres from its source in the Rocky Mountains to the beginning of the Fraser Valley at Hope, the Fraser River flows through a narrow river bed that is often constricted by canyons. Released from the Coast Mountains at Hope, it broadens out into a valley that is fifty kilometres wide by the time the Fraser debouches into the Strait of Georgia 160 kilometres to the west.

Over thousands of years, the Fraser has collected the debris of snow melt and erosion from its banks and tributaries. Over those same years, it has added these deposits to those left behind by retreating glaciers, forming an ever-growing delta and swelling the flood plain along the valley. By modern times, the river valley was thickly wooded, swampy, and subject to frequent flooding. Native Coast Salish peoples valued the teeming salmon runs; they established villages at the river's mouth and on higher ground, but stayed away from the mosquito-ridden swamps. The first newcomers to see the valley quickly found that much of the land could be farmed or settled only with much effort.

The arrival of the Canadian Pacific Railway in 1886 brought the first major change to the valley. By laying track to Burrard Inlet, the CPR created the new city of Vancouver and ensured that it would grow to dominate the province. From the turn of the century on, new settlers and governments drained and dyked the flood plain, making it suitable both for farming and for the building of new towns.

Railway and dykes were the key to the valley's potential. Vancouver expanded across the delta. The valley became more urban as cities and towns sprawled into farmland. Many predict that by 2010, the valley will house 3 million people, drawn by prosperity, the moderate climate, and the scenic beauty of mountain, ocean, and river.

It's anyone's guess whether Vancouver, Fraser, and their ilk would have approved. But it's almost certain that they did not foresee how dominant this region would become in British Columbia.

Opposite: *SeaBus, the double-ended passenger ferry that plies between North Vancouver and downtown Vancouver, heads towards Canada Place and the waterfront towers. Canada Place, with its striking Teflon-coated sails, was the Canadian Pavilion at Expo 86; it now serves as a trade and convention centre.*

Vancouver, 1896

In the 1890s, Li Hung Chang was described as the vice-roy of China, the Ambassador Extraordinary of the Emperor. Several thousand people crowded the docks to greet him on his arrival in Vancouver in 1896. Vancouver Chinese spent two thousand dollars on this triumphal arch and turned out in their finest clothes to see the ambassador ride by in a carriage drawn by four white horses.

The pageantry masked the strong anti-Oriental feelings of many a British Columbian. The first Chinese arrived in British Columbia to pan the sandbars and work the creeks in the Cariboo gold rush. Thousands came to help build the transcontinental railway in the 1880s; many stayed, to work in the cities, the logging camps, and the fish canneries. Though the province needed their labour, whites wanted them out, claiming that their culture was alien and that they took jobs from white men. Chinese lost the right to vote in 1874, were banned from government employment in 1878, and were made subject to a head tax in 1884. Li Hung Chang was asked to lobby against the head tax, but to no avail: it was raised in 1900, then raised again in 1903.

By then, there were some fifteen thousand Chinese in British Columbia. Twenty years later, faced with incessant lobbying from the British Columbia government, the federal government passed a law that effectively forbade Chinese immigration to Canada. Chinese-Canadians regained the right to vote only in 1947; immigration restrictions were lifted in the 1960s. (BCARS 9318)

Opposite: *The Symphony of Fire fireworks festival each summer attracts up to 400,000 spectators, who line the shoreline from West Vancouver to Point Grey to view the pyrotechnics. Local radio stations carry musical accompaniment to the spectacle. The fireworks are launched from barges in English Bay.*

Above: There has been an outdoor saltwater pool at Vancouver's Kitsilano Beach since the 1930s. The original was reduced by half in 1966, then replaced by this pool in 1979. The heated pool is open from approximately the Victoria Day weekend to Labour Day.

Opposite: Costumed celebrants welcome the Chinese New Year in the courtyard of the Chinese Cultural Centre. The gate in the background was built in China for Expo 86, and moved to Chinatown after the fair ended. The traditional Chinese New Year falls on the first new moon after the sun has entered the constellation of Aquarius in late January or early February.

Fraser River, 1910

Salmon was perhaps the most important resource for the native peoples of British Columbia long before whites arrived. It didn't take long for the newcomers to catch on: soon after the Hudson's Bay Company built Fort Langley on the lower Fraser River, company employees were salting and barrelling fish to be sent to England and the Sandwich Islands.

By 1910, when the gillnetters shown in the photograph above tied up at a Fraser River cannery, more than three thousand boats and scows and some ten thousand whites, natives, Chinese, and Japanese were employed in the fishing industry in the New Westminster district. The fishery was worth millions of dollars a year to the province; the twenty canneries on the Fraser River accounted for much of this production. Just a few years later, however, disaster struck: railway construction caused a rock slide in the Fraser Canyon, preventing large numbers of salmon from returning upstream and halving the number of fish that spawned in the Fraser. Fish ladders now help spawning salmon return home up the river. (BCARS 52933)

Opposite: *The skyline beyond Coal Harbour has grown in little more than a century from the few shacks and saloons that predated the arrival of the CPR to a forest of highrise office buildings and hotels. Development that started in 1993 will see new condominiums, apartments, retail space, and services built near the harbour shoreline.*

Above: A stainless-steel crab sculpture by George Norris raises its claws at the entrance to the Vancouver Museum and H.R. MacMillan Planetarium. The museum interprets Vancouver's human and natural history; in the planetarium, the stars speed by on universe-encompassing overhead screens.

Opposite: Dragon boats prepare to race in Vancouver's False Creek. At these races each June, paddlers compete to represent Canada at the dragon boat world championships in Hong Kong. The races honour a poet-statesman who drowned himself three thousand years ago. The geodesic dome in the background, built for Expo 86, contains Science World and an Omnimax theatre.

Port Moody, 1886

Port Moodyites had good reason to cheer when this first passenger train from Montreal reached their community on July 4, 1886. A thousand people came by boat from New Westminster, Victoria, and Nanaimo to join the celebration that marked the linking of the west and the east. But land speculators and residents alike already knew that Port Moody's fame would last little more than a day. The Canadian Pacific Railway had decided months before to extend the tracks to the infant city of Vancouver, where it would develop a deep-sea port to link the west coast to the Orient.

Such were the railway sweepstakes that saw one town thrive, another dwindle or die. The railway was the making of many a British Columbia town, not to mention many a speculator's fortune. Guess right about where the route would go and where the CPR would build a station, and you could be a millionaire. Guess wrong, and no one would even remember your name. Spurred by the railway, Vancouver grew from a collection of shanties and saloons by the waterfront to its present predominance in the west; spurned by the railway, Port Moody is now a pleasant residential town, an almost-suburb of Vancouver. (BCARS 11789)

Opposite: A former warehouse and industrial area, Granville Island, near the mouth of False Creek, has been transformed into a people place. Thousands throng the large public market, the specialty shops, the theatres and galleries, and the restaurants that overlook the many boats that moor nearby.

Above: The Stanley Park Causeway divides freshwater Lost Lagoon, once part of an inlet, from saltwater Coal Harbour. Created in 1886 in one of the first acts of the infant city council, 405-hectare Stanley Park is perhaps Vancouver's most zealously preserved green space.

Opposite: Cyclists pedal along the seawall past Siwash Rock in Vancouver's Stanley Park. Various Squamish native legends surround this fifteen-metre-tall rock. Each suggests the gods were impressed by a Squamish man who was purifying himself by swimming in the nearby waters, and transformed him into this rock.

Above: Thought to be the longest suspension bridge in the world, the Capilano Suspension Bridge reaches 137 metres across Capilano Canyon in North Vancouver. Built in 1956, this bridge, seventy metres above the river, is made of wire rope with wood decking. The first bridge at this point was built by native peoples of wood and hemp and called the "Laughing Bridge."

Opposite: The Point Atkinson lighthouse flashes its warning from a rocky headland on the West Vancouver shoreline, in Lighthouse Park. The first lighthouse tower was built here in 1874. This one dates from 1914; it is eighteen metres high, topped by a light that flashes thirty-three metres above the water.

Above: Visitors stroll the streets of Whistler Village at dusk. The village is the centre of Whistler Resort, north of Vancouver, several times voted North America's best ski resort. Whistler and Blackcomb mountains support twenty-seven ski lifts and more than two hundred runs, plus cross-country and heli-skiing, snowmobiling, and sleighing.

Opposite: Though it's better known as a winter ski resort, after the snow melts Whistler attracts many with its eighteen-hole golf course designed by Arnold Palmer. A second eighteen-hole course is being built on the lower slopes of Blackcomb Mountain, part of the Whistler-Blackcomb development.

Above: Flat areas north and south of the Fraser River were frequently flooded before dykes were built and boggy areas drained. Pitt Meadows, shown here, was lightly settled until Dutch immigrants who arrived after World War II drained and dyked the fields and settled down to grow berries, bulbs, and other produce.

Opposite: For thousands of years, the Fraser River rolled over land in the valley, leaving rich soil behind as it retreated. Once drained, the soil was ideal for farms such as this one. Dairying, small-fruit farming, and vegetable-growing are at the centre of the valley industry.

The Okanagan and Thompson Valleys

Manitoban John Moore Robinson was looking for gold when he rode up Okanagan Valley in 1890. But then he stopped one night at a lakeside homestead, where he ate some homegrown peaches for dessert. Right then and there—or so the story goes—he traded dreams of one pay streak for another: land that could produce such sweet and juicy fruit was surely land to make a fortune from.

Robinson went on to acquire, subdivide, and sell land in three areas he advertised as perfect Edens, founding in the process the towns of Summerland, Peachland, and Naramata. He was not the first, nor will he be the last, discoverer of the Okanagan, the largest and best-known of British Columbia's interior dry-belt valleys. Two hundred kilometres long and twenty kilometres wide, the Okanagan centres on a string of long narrow lakes, among them Okanagan, Kalamalka, Skaha, and Osoyoos. This and the Similkameen Valley to the west are dry and sunny, moderate in both climate and terrain.

The Okanagan Interior Salish gave their name to the valley, which translates aptly as "place of water." The first non-natives through the valley marvelled at the lush bunch grass that provided feed for their horses; by 1890, much of the valley was given over to cattle ranching. As Robinson discovered, the fertile glacial deposits on the sides and bottom of the valley could be put to better use. It took time to see his dream fully realized: only with the development of better varieties of fruit and efficient irrigation systems after World War I did the Okanagan become British Columbia's second most important agricultural region.

Recent years have seen the Okanagan's population swell with retired people and others who appreciate its sunny weather and small-town feeling. Kelowna is now B.C.'s third-largest city, with a population of seventy-five thousand; close to a quarter-million people live in the Okanagan Valley.

The Okanagan and Similkameen rivers are part of the Columbia River drainage basin. To the north, the Thompson River, a major tributary of the Fraser, drains the Shuswap, a wetter and more verdant valley. The Thompson then flows west into dry plateau lands, through Kamloops and Kamloops Lake, and turns south, collecting the waters of the Nicola valley before it joins the Fraser.

Lack of reliable transportation limited early success for Okanagan orchardists. The Shuswap and Thompson valleys were part of a different story. When the Canadian Pacific Railway built its transcontinental line through these valleys in the 1880s, towns grew up overnight. Kamloops, at the junction of the Thompson and North Thompson rivers, benefited the most—and did so again when the Northern Pacific was completed to the coast in 1915. It remains today the largest city in the central interior, a focal point for the cattle-ranching and logging country that surrounds it.

Though a traveller who visited the Okanagan twenty years before John Moore Robinson was referring only to that valley, his words ring true for all the valleys of the Thompson and Okanagan. "There is the making of happy homes for tens of thousands," he wrote. "In truth no more desireable country can be found."

Opposite: *An Okanagan orchard in bloom. Lord Aberdeen, owner of ranchland in the Okanagan and later Governor-General of Canada, planted the valley's first orchard in 1892. The Okanagan still produces apples, peaches, apricots, and other fruits, but orchard growers lament low prices, and some orchards are being ploughed under for housing developments and golf courses.*

Kelowna, 1910

"Another Eden Discovered in the West," trumpeted a 1900s magazine story in praise of the Okanagan Valley. "Fruit growing does not attract the lazy man," it continued, a truth that these apple pickers around 1910 near Kelowna could probably have affirmed. There was no room for the lazy in the routine of preparing land for an orchard, planting, irrigating, cultivating, spraying, picking, and protecting—not to mention marketing of the crop.

Between 1890 and 1914, land speculators and promoters sold off Okanagan land as fast as they could, citing the warm, dry climate, the long hours of sunshine, and the availability of water as ideal for fruit growing. Many planted orchards in those early years, and many failed: it was only with the development of reliable irrigation in the 1920s and 1930s that orcharding flourished. "Intelligent men do not pray for rain; they pay for rain," ran an oft-quoted slogan.

Some 95 per cent of British Columbia's apple crop is produced in the Okanagan Valley, together with apricots, peaches, and other tree fruits. (BCARS 22475)

Opposite: *At the north end of the Okanagan, the Vernon area receives more rain and is somewhat cooler than the south end of the valley. This farmstead overlooking Vernon, with its green meadows and trees, is typical of the area, which wooed early ranchers with bunch grass "higher than a horse's belly."*

Above: Kamloops is a city of bridges and rivers: the Thompson and North Thompson rivers converge here, to flow into Kamloops Lake to the west. The city, British Columbia's fifth largest, lives from logging and pulp and lumber production, mining, ranching, and its role as a service centre for surrounding territory.

Opposite: Grassy fields slope down to Okanagan Lake. The valley's long warm-water lakes, sunshine, and hot summer weather have made it one of British Columbia's most popular vacation sites. The moderate climate also attracts many retired people.

Above: The vineyards of Cedar Creek winery, near Kelowna, are among many that support a fast-growing industry. Since 1926, vintners have been planting grapes that thrive in the sunny, dry climate. Now, more than twenty wineries bottle wines that rank among the continent's best; many offer tours of the premises and wine tastings.

Opposite: Quiniscoe Lake, in remote Cathedral Lakes Provincial Park, southeast of Princeton and the Similkameen Valley. The park is a magnet for serious hikers and climbers, who value its stark and eroded rock formations and back-country beauty. Most trails start from the Quiniscoe Lake area.

Above: *The dry hills of the south Okanagan descend to the irrigated fields on the shores of Osoyoos Lake, in the south Okanagan. These arid hillsides receive less than thirty-five centimetres of rain each year, but irrigation water brought from lakes and streams in the hills transforms the land: in summer, fruit stands along the highways offer bounteous crops of cherries, apricots, peaches, plums, apples, tomatoes, melons, and grapes.*

Opposite: *Sagebrush and the yellow line-leaved daisy are among the dry-country plants that thrive in the Pocket Desert Ecological Reserve between Oliver and Osoyoos, in the south Okanagan. Known for its desert plants, such as the prickly pear cactus, this hundred-hectare reserve is also home to birds and animals such as turkey vultures, spadefoot toads, rattlesnakes, and various bats and amphibians.*

Salmon Arm, 1910

Whether mining town, logging town, or railway town, pioneer settlements in British Columbia closely resembled each other.

Along a muddy main street were built a row of false-fronted, wooden buildings: general store, post office, bank, saloon, hotel. Behind the businesses were the wooden houses of the first residents. Front Street in Salmon Arm, shown here in 1910, fit the pattern. Though trappers, gold miners, and would-be farmers joined the native Shuswap people from the 1820s on, the town was really a child of the Canadian Pacific Railway, which was laid through here in 1885.

Towns born of mining booms grew quickly and often died just as quickly. But Salmon Arm was not a boom town. It grew slowly, bolstered by the introduction of fruit farming in the 1890s. The first McGuire general store started in 1890; a second was opened five years later. From 1905 on, the settlement expanded as a dairying, fruit-growing, logging, and lumbering town. Just two years after this picture was taken, Salmon Arm was incorporated as a municipality. (BCARS 14335)

Opposite: *The Okanagan town of Oyama, named for a Japanese prince and field marshal, is built on the land bridge that separates Wood and Kalamalka lakes. The two were once known as Chelootsoos, "long lake cut in the middle." The brilliant greens of Kalamalka are attributed in legend to the Kalooey bears who swish their tails in the water and leave emerald pools behind.*

Above: Horses are still a familiar sight on the ranchland of the Nicola Valley, south of Kamloops. Much of the area east of Merritt is given over to ranching; the Douglas Lake Ranch is one of British Columbia's best known, and was for many years one of the largest in the world.

Opposite: The Murray Church at Nicola, east of Merritt, was built in 1876, after ranchers pre-empted land in the Nicola Valley and established a small community on Nicola Lake. Once the pre-eminent village in the valley, Nicola gave way to Merritt when coal mining began and a railway was built from Spences Bridge to Merritt.

The Rocky Mountains and West Kootenay

In 1985, the United Nations Educational, Scientific, and Cultural Organization declared the parks of Canada's Rocky Mountains a world heritage site. What UNESCO announced, Canadians and visitors from around the world already knew: Canada's Rockies contain some of the most magnificent scenery and most fascinating natural features in the world. Thrust up more than 50 million years ago as the earth's crust buckled and ruptured, then eroded and scraped by glaciers over thousands of years, the Rocky Mountains are everyone's first image when "Canada" comes to mind.

Even when the rail builders of the Canadian Pacific Railway were cursing and dynamiting their way through the mountains in the 1880s, they recognized the glory of the peaks and valleys that surrounded them. Almost as soon as the railway was complete, the CPR built mountain hotels and imported guides to serve the tourists that they knew would come from around the world.

The Rocky Mountains form the easternmost chain of peaks in British Columbia, the dividing line between the territories of the Plains Indians and Kutenai and Interior Salish peoples. They were the first steep barrier that faced explorers and settlers who came west from the prairies. In 1806, fur trader David Thompson cast about among the "stupendous solitary wilds" of the Rockies, seeking a pass that would lead him west, until the glorious day when he could declare, "by 10 a.m., we were at the head of the defile where the springs send their rills to the Pacific. This sight overjoyed me."

Today, the Rocky Mountains and the Rocky Mountain Trench, a long valley west of the mountains through which the Columbia River flows, are home to a few thousands who value both the beauty and the natural resources of the region. Many thousands more arrive every year, to hike, ski, watch wildlife, or just to appreciate the magnificence of both peaks and valley.

Residents of this region would not have been surprised if UNESCO had acknowledged a much larger area. West of the Columbia Valley, the Columbia Mountains rise in the Purcell, Selkirk, Monashee, and Cariboo ranges. Squeezed between the mountain chains are long, narrow lakes and river valleys, a scant portion of this mountainous region. Each successive range and valley seems more impressive than the previous one.

Called the West Kootenay because it is the western territory of the Kutenai Indians, it has been the provincial treasure chest since the 1890s. While British Columbia's gold rushes may have been more famous, the West Kootenay production of silver, lead, and zinc, and the smelting of ores in West Kootenay towns has probably been more significant.

Though the mines continue to produce and to sustain mining and smelting towns, the West Kootenay and Rocky Mountain regions are more and more seen as a different kind of treasure chest, of the type described by UNESCO. Even in a province crowded with peaks, these mountainous lands are something special.

Opposite: *Hikers look out over McArthur Lake in Yoho National Park. Hiking trails lead along creeks and mountain valleys to this lake and other attractions in Yoho, which takes its name from a Cree Indian word that expresses awe. The Burgess Shale, which contains fossils from 550 million years ago, is also in the park.*

Kaslo and Slocan Railway, Payne Bluff, 1890s

Mountains are picturesque highlights of a road or rail trip, less an obstacle than a delight. But British Columbia's mountainous terrain challenged those who built the roads and the railways. In this photograph, railway men pose in front of a wood-burning engine on the narrow-gauge Kaslo and Slocan Railway, at Payne Bluff, where the cliff rose sheer above them and dropped 330 metres straight down from the tracks.

Railway navvies carved the fifty-kilometre railway across the Slocan Range of the Selkirk Mountains, from Kootenay Lake to the 1890s silver-mining boom town of Sandon. A narrow-gauge spur line of the American Great Northern Railway, it was linked by steamer to a standard-gauge line that carried ore to smelters in the south.

The CPR saw the line as a threat, and an American-owned one at that, so the Canadian company built its own line from the west, to link up with CPR steamer service on Slocan Lake. The CPR built a depot in Sandon; K&S employees promptly wrecked it, claiming trespass. Locals cheered the K&S; it had, said one newspaper report, "sassed, bucked and licked the great, big Canadian Pacific to a fare-you-well." But the Canadian company eventually won: after the K&S was abandoned, the CPR laid a standard-gauge track that avoided the spectacular and dangerous bluff. (BCARS 5235)

Opposite: *Pink mimulus provides a summer foreground to Mount Robson, the highest peak in the Canadian Rockies.*

Above: Light and shadow sculpt Mount Assiniboine, in the south-central Rockies. The 3,618-metre peak, thrust up by folding and faulting of the earth's crust and eroded by glaciers, is the centrepiece of Mount Assiniboine Provincial Park, created in 1922 at the urging of the Alpine Club of Canada.

Opposite: Cross-country skiers tour below the peaks of Glacier National Park. Ski tourers must keep a careful eye on the weather here: Glacier, distinguished by its four hundred active glaciers and icefields, receives some of the heaviest snowfall in the province. Avalanches are a constant winter danger, and the park is scored by ancient and new avalanche paths.

Overleaf: Visitors look out over the Bugaboo Range, a mountaineering area in the north Purcells that attracts climbers from around the world. The Bugaboos were probably named when miners found a bugaboo, or dead-end mineral lead. Alpinists start their challenging climbs here before dawn, to avoid storms that often muscle in from the west in the afternoons.

Above: These fertile fields in the Creston Valley result from massive dyking and draining projects undertaken by government and private enterprise between the 1890s and 1930s. The dykes protect ten thousand hectares of farmland from the waters of the Kootenay River, which flooded the land every year. The remaining wetland is a waterfowl refuge, on the flyway followed by thousands of migrating birds.

Opposite: Lake O'Hara, in Yoho National Park, is an oasis in a sometimes busy mountain-park system. No private vehicles are allowed on the eleven-kilometre road to the lake. Visitors can hike in or take the bus (reservations required) to reach the lake, the mountains, the campsite, and the backcountry trails.

Overleaf: The two-thousand-kilometre-long Columbia River begins in the Rocky Mountains and flows north, then makes a mighty U-bend to flow south. Seen here near Revelstoke, the river has been greatly changed by hydroelectric dams. The Mica and Revelstoke dams, both near Revelstoke, hold back reservoirs north of town.

Above: In the 1890s, miners flocked to the West Kootenay, and a score of mining towns grew up. Nelson lasted longer than most; a service and government centre for the mining camps, it was built of brick and stone. Heritage buildings on Baker Street, shown here, are part of a well-preserved and restored turn-of-the-century streetscape.

Opposite: Scarlet paintbrush and Arctic lupines are among the alpine flowers that carpet this meadow in Mount Revelstoke National Park. Alpine meadows in the park are among the few in Canada accessible by road. The more energetic can follow a trail to the summit, then continue on by foot to remote mountain lakes and creeks.

Mount Robson, 1913

As three of their number made the first successful assault on Mount Robson, highest peak in the Canadian Rockies, in the summer of 1913, these members of the Alpine Club of Canada conducted other climbs and explorations in the Mount Robson area.

Founded in 1906, the alpine club held yearly summer camps for its members. Unlike the British Alpine Club, after which it was modelled, the Canadian club accepted women members, who soon became some of the most sure-footed of climbers. At first, they followed the fashion of the times, wearing long skirts that caught on bushes and slowed them as they toiled uphill. But Swiss and Austrian guides, imported by the Canadian Pacific Railway and by the alpine club, persuaded them to tuck their petticoats into their bloomers, or, better yet, to wear the knickerbockers visible in this photograph.

After 1885, mountaineering attracted many to British Columbia's mountains. A comment from W.W. Foster, who with Albert MacCarthy and guide Conrad Kain made that successful climb of Mount Robson, suggests why: "We beheld a sea of mountains, glaciers, snowfields, lakes and waterways, displayed in endless array . . . . but a tithe of the country's vast scenic heritage." (BCARS 99265)

Opposite: *Old buildings and machinery at Fort Steele Provincial Heritage Park, near Cranbrook. Fort Steele began as Galbraith's Ferry, a town on the Kootenay River that served nearby mining camps in the 1860s. When a railway depot was built at Cranbrook, Fort Steele declined. With restored and re-created buildings from here and elsewhere in the region, it is a major heritage attraction.*

The North Coast

It's easy to be envious of the Victorian era, when purple prose and endless adjectives were essential contents of the travel writer's suitcase. How, for example, to better the words written in 1892 by a voyager up British Columbia's coast:

"Breathing the very air of Heaven itself, you burst, like the Ancient Mariner, into an unknown sea filled with untold beauties, and sail over a bosom of waters as unruffled as glass; among myriads of islands; through deep, rugged, rock-walled channels; past ancient Indian villages, medieval glaciers, dark solemn, pine-clothed shores, snow-capped peaks, dashing cataracts, yawning mountain gorges, spouting monsters and sea whelps."

But in a terser age, perhaps two facts suffice. The coast of British Columbia, measured in a direct line from north to south, is a thousand kilometres long. The coast of British Columbia, measured in all its fjords, islands, bays, and capes, is some thirty thousand kilometres long.

Like the rest of B.C., this serrated, indented coast is a product of ancient geological forces. A long-ago buckling of the earth's crust sank deep troughs and uplifted and folded mountain ranges along what is now the coast. The sea advanced and retreated and advanced. Erupting volcanoes and earthquakes shifted and shaped the land and seafloor. Ice spread out along almost every part of the coast, then melted, scouring, scraping, and eroding, to produce the characteristic valleys, inlets, and mountains that are so spectacular today.

Two centuries ago, the coast was one of the most populated parts of the region, with native settlements on inlet, river mouth, and island. The coast was—and is—the realm of the Haida, Bella Bella, Heiltsuk, Tsimshian, and Kwakwaka'wakw peoples, who used land trails to trade with other peoples, but who turned their faces mainly to the sea.

Early explorers also came by sea. Fishers, loggers, and settlers lived in villages and camps all along the coast. But, as the twentieth century advanced, people depended less and less on the sea. Airplanes replaced ferries; roads replaced sea lanes. People were less content to live in the relative isolation of the coast. The coast today supports fewer settlements, and fewer people outside the rare towns, than it did fifty years ago.

And that is part of its continuing charm. On the map, just three red road lines lead overland from the B.C. interior to the coast. Along the entire length of the mainland coast between the Lower Mainland and Prince Rupert, there are just four major settlements: Powell River, Bella Bella, Bella Coola, and Kitimat. Though logging and mining roads honeycomb parts of the Queen Charlottes, the islands have just one public highway.

This remoteness and beauty have called forth the talents of people who, like that 1892 panegyrist, want to see preserved "the purest, the rarest, the wildest, the most beautiful, and the grandest forms of nature."

Opposite: *Fishing boats tie up at Prince Rupert docks. Known as the Halibut Capital of the World, Prince Rupert, with a population of 16,600 by far the largest city on the north coast, has long been home port for many north-coast commercial fishers. Fish canneries were once clustered at the mouth of the Skeena River, and before World War II, special fish trains ran several times a week to take salmon to the Prairies and the American midwest.*

Bella Coola, 1873

In 1873, provincial Superintendent of Indian Affairs Dr. Israel Wood Powell disembarked from HMS *Boxer* at Bella Coola, an isolated coastal settlement, and posed with fellow passengers and crew in front of the Nuxalk village.

Like many coastal villages, this one had been touched by contact with whites, but was still relatively unchanged. When Alexander Mackenzie crossed the Coast Mountains on his way to the sea in 1792, he entered the territory of the Nuxalk, who fed him, lent him canoes, and supplied paddlers that Mackenzie said were the best he had ever seen.

Though fur traders stopped at Bella Coola and the Hudson's Bay Company opened a post, there were still few white settlers eighty years after Mackenzie's visit. The village remained a row of plank-sided houses, some built on pilings that raised them above the tidal flats, with connecting plank sidewalks. Prominent on the riverbank in this photograph are basket-like fish traps, made from reeds or roots. The traps were suspended just below the tops of weirs the Nuxalk built across the river in summer and fall.

In 1894, Norwegian settlers arrived in Bella Coola, accelerating the process of change. The town of seven hundred is now a mixture of Nuxalk and non-native. (BCARS 57598)

Opposite: *The rugged Queen Charlotte Mountains are the spine of the Queen Charlotte Islands, descending from their 1,100-metre summits abruptly on the steep and indented west coast, more gently on the east. This photograph shows why the islands are also known as "The Misty Isles."*

Above: Sports fishers reel in salmon near Kano Inlet, on the west coast of Graham Island, in the Queen Charlotte Islands. A number of fly-in fishing camps are based in the Charlottes, a fact that sometimes causes friction with the native Haida, who resent outsiders taking a resource they consider the Haida should regulate in the land they call Haida Gwaii.

Opposite: This moss-covered totem was carved by a Checleset Nuu-chah-nulth native of cedar, the tree that sustained this seafaring nation. Like other coastal native peoples, they travelled by cedar canoe, built their houses of cedar, wove baskets of cedar roots, and used cedar in almost every aspect of their daily lives.

Overleaf: One could forgive Captain George Vancouver, exploring these waters in 1792, who so-named Desolation Sound because the dark and silent forests, the steep shores, and the deep inlet left him and his crew forlorn. But today's boaters are delighted by the sense of solitude and beauty of the sound, north of Powell River.

Above: ''Perhaps an atheist could view it and remain an atheist,'' wrote mystery novelist Earle Stanley Gardner of Princess Louisa Inlet, pictured here, ''but I doubt it.'' An international society owns and has vowed to preserve part of the north shore of the inlet, at the head of Jervis Inlet, one of the coast's narrow, scenic, and deep-sided fjords.

Opposite: A traveller cruising the Inside Passage drops anchor near Princess Royal Island, south of Prince Rupert. Princess Royal is one of the largest islands along the Inside Passage, interconnected straits and channels that weave a protected waterway between Desolation Sound and Prince Rupert.

Overleaf: High in the Coast Range south of Bella Coola, a glacial pond lies below mountain peaks. The characteristic steel-grey of the glacier above the pond occurs when successive layers of new snow and older tiny ice crystals squeeze air out of the ice crystals below.

The Cariboo–Chilcotin

When people think of the wild west of myth and movie, they see cowboys and cattle, sagebrush and dusty trails, weathered wood and listing log cabins. But the picture frame is always space: rolling hills and endless expanses under the sun of a prairie sky.

Almost any western movie could have been set in the Cariboo-Chilcotin, a broad, dry, right-angled triangle of plateau in south-central British Columbia, bordered on the west by the peaks and glaciers of the Coast Mountains, on the north by pine forests, and on the east by the Quesnel Highlands and Cariboo Mountains.

But when you think about the wild west, somehow the word "featureless" creeps in, and that's where the Cariboo-Chilcotin departs from legend. This wide plateau, shaped and eroded by slow-moving glacial ice and by relentless rivers that have cut deep channels, is nowhere quite flat and everywhere quite surprising.

The Cariboo-Chilcotin is two regions, divided by the Fraser River. East of the Fraser and west of the Cariboo Mountains lies the Cariboo. Long the home of Shuswap and Carrier natives, this area gained fame throughout the western world after 1859, when prospectors followed gold creeks from the plateau into the hills and found the mother lode east of present-day Quesnel.

The Cariboo gold rush precipitated great change: by the late 1860s, more than ten thousand people lived in the gold towns, a road had been built north along the Fraser River and across the plateau, native trails had been upgraded to roads, steamers ran on the lakes and rivers, and ranchers herded cattle on great grassland stretches. Though the Cariboo grew a little quieter once the gold was mined out, the changes were irrevocable. Today's Cariboo still supports cattle ranches, loggers who mine the lodgepole-pine forests, and tourist-camp operators who have seen the potential of ghost towns, quiet lakes, and rushing rivers.

The Chilcotin is a different world. Beyond the Fraser, it was almost untouched by the gold rush; only slowly has the frontier shifted west. The one road that crosses the Chilcotin was not completed until 1951, and part remains unpaved. In this region, native Tsilqot'in and non-native peoples each make up half the population.

Though the Chilcotin contains the requisite rolling ranchland and wide-open spaces, it is much more than that. The Fraser and Chilcotin rivers have gouged deep beds; they run in many places a hundred metres below the benchlands, flanked by hoodoos and wind-eroded canyon walls. Some of the province's most beautiful lakes lie in the western Chilcotin, long blue expanses that reflect the Coast Mountains.

As befits a region that has a wild-west reputation to uphold, the Cariboo-Chilcotin is still a land of individualists who resolutely refuse to fit into any mould. Neither they nor the land will ever be termed featureless.

Opposite: *The Rainbow Range, part of the eastern flank of the Coast Mountains, is aptly named: purple, red, and yellow mineralization colours the rock bluffs and scree slopes. The mountains, which rise to twenty-five hundred metres, are visible from the Chilcotin Highway northwest of Anahim Lake.*

Above: A Beaver aircraft taxis on Spruce Lake in the south Cariboo. The Beaver, a high-winged, single-engined plane, has often been called the workhorse of the north. First built in 1947, the long-serving Beavers have carried freight and passengers into and out of the most remote and roughest areas of British Columbia.

Opposite: Weathered wooden buildings, such as this barn near Little Fort north of Kamloops, dot the Cariboo. Log cabins, old roadhouses, barns, elegant silvered ranch houses—some abandoned, some still occupied, some restored as historic sites—testify to the region's history.

Previous pages: Paddlers strike out along Isaac Lake, the longest of the six major lakes that, together with smaller lakes, streams, and portages, form the 116-kilometre Bowron Lakes canoe circuit in the northeast Cariboo. The roughly rhomboidal circuit charms canoeists with its views of the lakes, the Cariboo Mountains, and the wildlife along its shores.

Barkerville, mid-1860s

Gold! Gold on the Fraser River, gold in the Cariboo. That was the cry that resounded from San Francisco to the Canadas to Europe between 1858 and the mid-1860s, causing people to throw up their jobs and take ship for British Columbia. By the time pioneer photographer Frederick Dally took this picture of its main street in the mid-1860s, Barkerville, gold rush capital of the Cariboo, had a population estimated at more than ten thousand: prospectors, miners, teamsters, merchants, saloon keepers, dancing girls, gamblers—anyone who thought he or she could make a living from the mines or from the miners.

Almost all of these wooden buildings burned when fire raced down the street in 1868. Barkerville was rebuilt, but the lustre was gone from the gold rush, for the hard-rock mining needed to reach the gold that remained required not just enthusiasm, but also capital.

The results of the rush lasted longer than the town did. The Fraser and Cariboo rushes brought the area to the world's attention. The mainland colony of British Columbia was created because of the gold rush, shoring up Britain's claim to the region. A road was built into the interior, ranchers began the cattle-raising industry that still dominates the Cariboo, and many Chinese entered the province, to share in the gold. Barkerville is now a restored ghost town. (BCARS 10109)

Opposite: Main Street in the restored Cariboo gold rush town of Barkerville.

Above: Cattle such as these have ranged the Cariboo benches since the first ranchers came to feed prospectors on their way to Cariboo gold in the 1860s. Some of the largest cattle ranches in the world cover vast stretches of the region.

Above: The interior plateau lies in British Columbia's dry belt, with precipitation as little as two hundred millimetres a year. To grow crops or cattle fodder such as that shown here near Cache Creek, ranchers and farmers must irrigate, bringing water up from the Thompson River or down from lakes and streams in the surrounding hills.

Overleaf: Hikers look out over sixty-five-kilometre-long Chilko Lake in the Chilcotin. Long praised for its beauty, Chilko Lake is now part of Ts'yl-os Provincial Park, a 1994 addition to the B.C. parks system—and an innovation, for it is managed jointly by the parks branch and the Nemiah Valley Tsilqot'in Band.

The North

An oil rig pumps up and down in a field of ripening wheat. A helicopter buzzes back and forth over a landscape of muskeg and mountains, its equipment tracing maps for geologists to decipher. In the morning sun below the shadowed peak of Stekyawden, native hands carefully create a modern carving in an ancient tradition.

Three images so disparate that they seem to belong to three different lands. And in a sense they do: British Columbia's north is fully half the province and as varied as British Columbia itself.

Part of this region lies between the Rocky Mountains and the Alberta border, the only part of B.C. east of the Rockies and the only part that drains north to the Arctic rather than west to the Pacific. This area just west of the 120th parallel of longitude and south of the sixtieth parallel of latitude is British Columbia only by an accident of history, appended to B.C. by the British government before Alberta existed.

But for years, the region has looked east to the Prairies rather than south to B.C. It shares a time zone with Alberta; a road and a railway snaked west from Alberta long before any were built north from B.C.; and at one point Peace River residents petitioned to be allowed to join Alberta. The Peace River country is prairie land, part of the northernmost grain-growing area on the continent. The grain fields are dotted with oil wells: the sedimentary basin that covers most of Alberta and Saskatchewan extends into northeast B.C., the only part of the province where oil and natural gas are found.

North of Peace River country, spruce, pine, and birch forests take over, and muskeg replaces more solid ground. In 1942, Canadian workers and American soldiers built the Alaska Highway north through this land to the Yukon and Alaska; that road, which climbs gradually into the northern Rockies, is still a symbol of wilderness and adventure for many who drive it.

South of the Peace, west of the Rockies, the north's main transportation corridor cuts across the province from Alberta border to Pacific Ocean. Road and rail follow this corridor through Prince George, population seventy thousand, known as B.C.'s northern capital. Like towns to east and west, this city lives from logging, lumbering, and pulp mills.

North of the road and rail is a wilderness of lakes, rivers, mountains, and muskeg. This is the land of the Dene, of fishers and hunters, of old prospectors who still seek gold along remote creeks, and of new prospectors who map ore-bearing bodies from the air.

West again, road and rail rise towards the Coast Mountains, crossing from the traditional territory of the interior Carrier people into that of the Tsimshian and Tahltan coastal peoples. This region along the border of the Alaska Panhandle contains some of the province's most magnificent scenery: the lava fields of the Nass River, the barren multi-coloured beauty of Mount Edziza, the glacial wilderness and abundant wildlife of the Spatsizi, and the blue reaches of Atlin Lake—images almost foreign to those of wheatfields and oil wells, but still very much a part of British Columbia's north.

Opposite: *Fireweed fronts the mountains of the Tatlatui Range some two hundred kilometres north of Hazelton. The spectacular mountain landscape here is heavily eroded by glaciers that scraped the peaks and scoured the valleys ten thousand and more years ago.*

Dease Lake, 1925

In 1925, this Vickers Viking flying boat flew a prospecting party here to Dease Lake, in British Columbia's northwest. Chartered and shipped by rail to Prince Rupert by an American mining syndicate, the plane was reassembled, then flown in stages to Wrangell, Telegraph Creek, and finally to Dease Lake. Throughout the summer, the prospectors surveyed the area, the first aerial mineral exploration in western Canada.

Since they found no major deposits, the expedition's importance was more symbolic than real, an indication of the changes that air transport would bring. Since the beginning of human habitation in the north, people had moved on foot, on horseback, and by canoe across the truly vast expanses of forest, muskeg, lakes, and rivers of the north. Travel was slow and often arduous.

The coming of the airplane transformed life in the north. Pioneering bush pilots could go almost anywhere in a fraction of the time such journeys would take by land. Planes brought isolated native communities into much quicker and closer touch with the cities. And in the tradition of that first flight, prospectors in helicopters and bush planes now survey thousands of square kilometres of territory every summer. (BCARS 91730)

Opposite: Hikers look out over Crater Lake, just below 1,065-metre Chilkoot Pass in B.C.'s northwest corner. Close to a hundred years ago, thousands of heavily laden prospectors struggled up to the pass and on to the Klondike gold fields by way of this Chilkoot Trail. Today, hikers from around the world follow the fifty-three-kilometre trail from Dyea, Alaska, to Bennett, British Columbia.

Above: The MV Tarahne, *restored and at rest by the shore of Atlin Lake, in northwest* B.C. The Tarahne *sailed the lake from 1917 to 1936 for the White Pass and Yukon Railway, carrying freight and passengers between lakeshore settlements. In 1927, the boat was hauled ashore, cut in two, and a nine-metre section built in the middle.*

Above: This windmill on a farm in the Peace River Valley underlines the region's links with the Prairies, where wind power has long been used to generate farm electricity. B.C.'s Peace River farming belt produces crops more commonly associated with the Prairie provinces: wheat, barley, and other grains.

Overleaf: The yellow fields of canola, near Dawson Creek, are a sight repeated across the Canadian prairies. Canada has led development of canola products—oil, meal, and seed that come from the rape plant. Considered nutritionally superior to oils containing more saturated fats, canola, used in Asia for thousands of years, is now popular in North America and Europe.

PHOTO CREDITS

D. Baswick/First Light p. 72

Trevor Bonderud/First Light pp. 5, 17, 47

Michael E. Burch pp. 6-7, 8, 14, 18, 28-29, 31, 32-33, 36-37, 40, 40-41, 42, 46, 51, 54, 55, 65, 89

(C) A. Griffiths/First Light p. 26

Chris Harris/First Light pp. 58-59, 86-87, 92

Richard Hartmier/First Light p. 100

Al Harvey pp. 2-3, 4, 9, 38, 39, 48-49, 49, 52-53, 68, 74-75, 77, 78-79, 82-83, 88, 90-91, 94-95, 96, 98-99, 101

Joseph S. King pp. 24-25, 34

Thomas Kitchin/First Light pp. viii, 20-21, 35, 37, 66-67, 69, 93

J. A. Kraulis pp. 62-63

Patrick Morrow/First Light p. 30

David Nunuk/First Light pp. 12-13, 15, 16-17, 19

Jason Puddifoot/First Light pp. 76, 80

John Sylvester/First Light pp. 10-11, 44-45

Steve Short/First Light pp. 50, 60, 61, 64, 81, 84, 102-103

Alan Sirulnikoff/First Light pp. vi-vii

Ron Watts/First Light pp. 22, 27, 56

Darwin R. Wiggett/First Light pp. 70-71

All archival photographs are courtesy of the British Columbia Archives and Records Service.

AQUARIUM FISH

A PORTRAIT OF THE ANIMAL WORLD

Andrew Cleave

NEW LINE BOOKS

Fax: (888) 719-7723
e-mail: info@newlinebooks.com

Printed and bound in Korea

ISBN 1-59764-074-3

Visit us on the web!
www.newlinebooks.com

PHOTO CREDITS

Photographer/Page Number

E.R. Degginger 10, 11 (bottom), 14, 15, 18, 20, 22, 24-25, 26, 27 (top & bottom), 28 (top & bottom),
29, 30 (top & bottom), 31 (top and bottom) 32, 33, 34, 35 (top & bottom), 36-37, 38 (top & bottom),
39 (top & bottom), 40 (top & bottom), 41 (top & bottom), 42, 43, 44 (top & bottom), 45, 46 (top & bottom) 47

Tom Stack & Associates
Mike Bacon 54, 66
Gerald & Buff Corsi 52, 64-65
Dave B. Fleetham 12, 62
Gary Milburn 70 (top)
Randy Morse 6
Brian Parker 16, 21, 23, 55, 70 (bottom)
Mike Severns 50
Denise Tackett 7, 63
Larry Tackett 8-9, 13, 17, 71

The Wildlife Collection
Chris Huss 3, 4, 5, 11 (top), 19 (top), 48-49, 51 (top & bottom), 53, 56, 57 (top & bottom), 58, 59, 60, 61, 67, 68, 69
Dean Lee 19 (bottom)

INTRODUCTION

Who could dispute this fish's claim to being the queen angelfish, Holacanthus ciliaris*? The electric-blue markings of the juveniles are replaced by vibrant golds and yellows as the fish matures.*

Man has kept fish in captivity for almost as long as he has recorded history. The ancient Romans raised fish in ponds and tanks, though these creatures were destined not to be cared for as pets, but for the table. The city of Naples was noted for its elaborate system of ponds, both freshwater and marine, which were home to many large, and presumably edible, fish. It was probably the Chinese, however, who first kept ornamental fish, about one thousand years ago. Their favorite was the goldfish, which they kept in large bowls or opaque tanks (goldfish look attractive from above, so the lack of glass aquaria made little difference). The Japanese also enjoyed keeping goldfish, and perfected the art of breeding them in strange and beautiful colors.

By the middle of the seventeenth century goldfish had been introduced into Europe, but were still kept in bowls or ponds and viewed only from above. Many varieties were available, all of which looked interesting from above, with their bright colors, strangely shaped heads, and flowing fins; the more bizarre they appeared, they more popular they were.

By the middle of the nineteenth century, relatively cheap glass aquaria had been developed and more fish species were available to collectors. Amateur fish-keeping was still a somewhat expensive privilege of the upper classes, but many homes had one or two goldfish which they kept in bowls. Public aquaria were established in Britain and on the Continent, and some of the earliest books on the subject

In the aquarium the Achilles tang, Acanthurus achilles, can be very particular about its dietary requirements. Encouraging algae to grow in the aquarium will allow this fish to graze among rocks and corals, much as it does in its natural marine habitat.

were published. And other fish-keeping techniques were invented in Britain to enable naturalists to keep cold-water marine species healthy for prolonged periods of study.

Toward the end of the nineteenth century, numerous species of tropical fish were brought to Europe and became extremely popular. Their great variety of colors and shapes, and the ease with which they could be kept, soon led them to become the most common fish collected in aquaria. Goldfish continued to be popular, but were more likely to be seen out of doors in ponds.

The earliest aquarists had quite a struggle to keep their pets alive without the benefit of electricity, thermostatically controlled heaters, efficient filtration systems, and the means to accurately test water for chemical imperfections. But the constant fascination of fish-keeping ensured that a consistent effort was made to find answers to these problems, so that today fish-keeping is a widespread and very popular hobby. Modern aquarists have a great deal of highly technical equipment available to them, and well over a hundred years of expertise and experience to draw on.

Today there is also an immense variety of fish available to the amateur aquarist. Tropical freshwater species are still the most popular, but cold-water aquarium fish like the goldfish, found in a great range of colors and forms, are still very widely kept. Saltwater aquaria present more problems than freshwater, but with the great advances in equipment design in recent years, tropical marine fish—plus organisms like anemones, prawns, and corals—can be kept by a reasonably skilled amateur. Cold-water marine species can be kept successfully, too, provided the correct equipment is available.

Once established, most aquaria require a minimum of upkeep and will enhance any room. A well-maintained aquarium with a healthy community of fish and a good growth of aquatic plants can also provide hours of interest and stimulus for further study; many interesting discoveries have been made by amateur aquarists pursuing their hobby. In fact, observing fish in an aquarium often leads to the even more rewarding study of fish in their natural environment.

These brightly colored maroon clownfish, or anemone fish, (Premnas biaculeatus), are one of several related species. All are similar in appearance and make an interesting addition to the smaller marine aquarium.

THE AQUATIC VERTEBRATES

Fish are classified as vertebrates—animals with backbones. One group, the sharks and rays, have skeletons made of cartilage, but all other fish have skeletons composed of bone. This supports the muscles and protects some of the organs, such as the brain and spinal cord.

Anatomy

The great bulk of the body of a fish is made up of muscle; the space occupied by internal organs is small compared to that of mammals. These muscles are used to flex the body from side to side to enable the fish to swim. It is the tail which provides propulsion; the smaller fins are used to stabilize the body and help the fish to steer and avoid danger. The dorsal fin, on the back, and the small pelvic and ventral fins on the underside, stop the fish rolling from side to side as it moves forward, and the paired pectoral fins at the front can be extended to help the fish stop quickly.

Most of the bony fish have a body covering of scales—thin, overlapping bony plates—which protect the skin beneath, help to streamline the body, and act as a flexible armor which enables the fish to be active without restricting its movement. In some fish the scales are very small, few in number, deeply embedded in the skin, or absent, but most species have a full body armor. The outer surface of a fish is covered with a layer of mucus, giving the fish a slimy feel. This mucus helps protect the body of the fish from external parasites or attacks by fungal diseases, and is also a further form of streamlining. It is very important when handling fish that the mucus not be wiped off, as this can leave the fish vulnerable to disease.

The mouths of fish are adapted to their way of life. Some have tiny mouths and no teeth, while others have large, gaping mouths and fearsome arrays of powerful teeth. Fish are unable to chew their food, but they can bite chunks from it, and some have tooth-like structures in their throats which help them grind up their meals.

The swim bladder—a gas-filled bladder deep inside the body—is a vital organ which acts as a buoyancy tank to help the fish

Following page: The Oriental sweet-lips' (Plectorhynchus orientalis) large size and huge mouth hide the fact that this is a shy fish with the habit of eating only tiny morsels of food.

The long-nosed hawk-fish, Oxycirrhites typus, is an agile predator, albeit of very small prey. Much of its time is spent motionless on suitable promonto-ries from which it can dart out and snatch unsuspecting prey.

The tiny size and elongated shape of this diamond blenny, Malacoctenus boehlkei, enable it to take up residence in the most limited of spaces. These terr-itories are valiantly defended against even the largest trespassers.

maintain its position in the water. Some species, particularly those which spend most of their time on the bottom, lack the swim bladder, and have some difficulty in swimming up to the surface. A few species can use their swim bladders to help produce grunting or clicking sounds.

Being permanently immersed in water, fish always run a risk of absorbing too much fluid. The kidneys, therefore, which are proportionately larger in fish than in other vertebrates, are also very important organs, responsible for maintaining the correct balance of water in the fish's body. A few specialized fish—particularly migrant species like eels and salmon—have kidneys which can cope with variable salinity, and so are able to live in both fresh and salt water, but these species are unsuitable for aquaria. Most fish are unable to make this switch; if they are put in the wrong type of water, they die very quickly.

Fish obtain oxygen through their gills, the red comb-like structures at the back of the mouth. Each fish has two sets of gills protected by bony flaps on either side of the head; when these are open it is sometimes possible to glimpse the gills inside them. Water, bearing dissolved oxygen, flows through the mouth and passes over the gills, where the oxygen is taken into the blood stream and carbon dioxide is released. The gills look red because they have a rich supply of blood vessels covered by a very thin membrane. As a fish swims along, apparently "drinking" water, it is really breathing by taking in a fresh supply of oxygen-rich water every time it opens its mouth. Some fish use this process to help them feed as well, filtering the water through much tougher, comb-like structures called gill rakers to remove tiny food particles or small organisms. A few fish can breathe by gulping air from the surface of the water into specialized organs which act like lungs; these species normally live in habitats where the water is very low in oxygen.

Environmental Adaptations

Fish are found in almost every type of watery habitat from the depths of the oceans, the open sea, and the seashore, to freshwater lakes, rivers, and ponds. They live in the coldest polar waters and the warmest tropical seas and rivers. Most require clean water, but some are tolerant of poor conditions and low oxygen levels. Fish exhibit many different adaptations to their habitats; while all have the same basic structures, there is a vast variety of shapes, sizes, and colors.

Fish of the open sea and those which live in large, fast-flowing rivers have what we think of as the classic fish shape: a well-proportioned body and a normal arrangement of fins. Many have rather plain coloring since they have no need for markings to camouflage them against a background. Many fish that normally spend their time swimming in open water can take food from the top or the bottom, simply by being good swimmers.

Those species that live on the bottom have flattened bodies with coloring that matches the surface they lie on, but their undersides, which remain hidden, are usually plain. Bottom-dwellers' mouths are directed downwards to facilitate feeding, and they often

This unusually named porkfish, Amisotremus virginicus, is part of a family of fishes commonly called grunts. By grinding their pharyngeal teeth, these fish are able to produce sounds audible to the human ear.

have barbels around the mouth to help them locate food in the mud below them. Fish that feed on the surface, however, have mouths designed to point upwards, so they can take in food without having to push too much of their body out of the water.

Fish that live in fast-moving rivers, such as trout, are often slender and streamlined to cope with the strong current. When put into an aquarium they become very restless, spending much of their time swimming rapidly around the tank. They also require high levels of oxygen and low temperatures,

Since its introduction to the aquarium trade, the scientific name of the ram, Microgeophagus ramirezi, has changed several times as a result of increasing knowledge of this delicate little fish's biology.

so may not be very suitable in a tank with other fish in it. Some fish that live in fast rivers, though, have flattened bodies to enable them to live on the bottom without being swept away by the current; these may be more suitable subjects for the aquarium.

Species that live in still water exhibit still other adaptations to their environment. While these types of fish are not in danger of being swept away by the current, they may be vulnerable to attacks by other fish, so camouflage is often quite important. Some have markings which look striking when isolated in an aquarium, but help the fish to blend in with surrounding vegetation in their natural habitat. Many fish have vertical stripes which make them attractive to the human eye, but these markings actually serve to help the fish merge visually with the stems of reeds or pond weeds. Likewise, fish with thin bodies can swim easily between plant stems, but when viewed from the side they have a distinctive

appearance which makes them a good choice for an aquarium.

While camouflage is important to many fish, the need for cryptic markings is sometimes superseded by the need to attract a mate or warn off a rival. Fish that are able to escape from danger easily or ward off predators by attacking them can usually afford to have bright colors and striking body shapes. In some species, it is only the males which have the elaborate body forms or colors, while the females have more subdued markings. Many young fish lack the distinctive appearance of the adults. Because they are small and inexperienced, they need extra protection in order to survive; until they reach their full size they have markings which help them hide from danger. Although to human eyes some features may appear to be unnecessarily elaborate or extravagantly colored, they have developed that way over the course of thousands of years of slow evolution to suit the individual species and its way of life.

The large aquarium and continuous supply of live food required by fish such as this dragon moray eel, **Muraena pardalis,** *make keeping species like this a possibility only for enthusiastic specialists and public aquaria.*

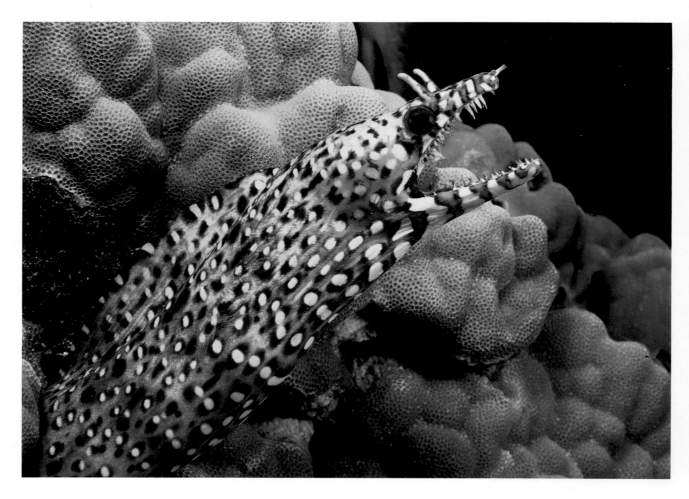

Senses

The fish's most important sense organ is the lateral line. In many species this can be seen quite clearly, looking like a line of dots running along either side of the body from head to tail. These dots are actually linked to sensitive nerve endings which are, in turn, connected to a fluid-filled canal beneath the skin. The lateral line is sensitive to pressure changes in the water, and helps the fish maintain an awareness of movement close to its body.

Most species are able to see well in color; in fact, fish themselves are often very colorful. They sometimes produce these colors to act as warnings or to attract mates, so their good color vision is therefore quite necessary to their survival.

The sense of smell is also very well developed in some fish, especially those which live in dark conditions or muddy water. Catfish, for example, have long, sensitive whiskers, and can find their food easily in the muddiest of water.

Reproduction

With a few exceptions, fish reproduce by laying eggs. Some species fertilize their eggs internally and the females carry the developing eggs inside their bodies, but most fish fertilize their eggs outside the body. Fish have paired reproductive organs inside their bodies which produce the sperm, or milt, in the males, and the eggs, or ova, in the females.

Mating, or spawning, often takes place as a group activity in shoaling fish species; vast numbers of eggs and sperm are shed into the water at once. Most of the eggs are fertilized, but some are eaten by the fish which produced them and any others in the vicinity. Fortunately, so many fertilized eggs are produced that many escape being eaten and hatch into tiny babies, or fry. Many of these are also eaten by fish and other predators, but once again, a few of the large number which hatch will escape predation and survive to become adults.

Once the eggs have been laid and fertilized, most species of fish take no further interest in

Gobies such as this elegant fire goby, Nemateleotris decora, share many similar habits with blennies, but there is no mistaking the gaudy colors that provide the gobies with perfect camouflage against the soft corals of shallow reefs.

them. Some fall to the riverbed and settle between stones or gravel, where they remain until they hatch, while others are sticky and adhere to plants or tree roots in the water. A few fish take more trouble with their eggs; these species usually lay far fewer than those which scatter them at random. Some make small nests to protect the eggs, and guard them until the young hatch; predators are warned away and the nest is kept clean. Other fishes' eggs are stuck to stones and watched over, and some even incubate the eggs inside their mouths. Once hatched, the fry are protected until they can fend for themselves; sometimes the parent keeps its young near the nest, or even shelters them inside its mouth.

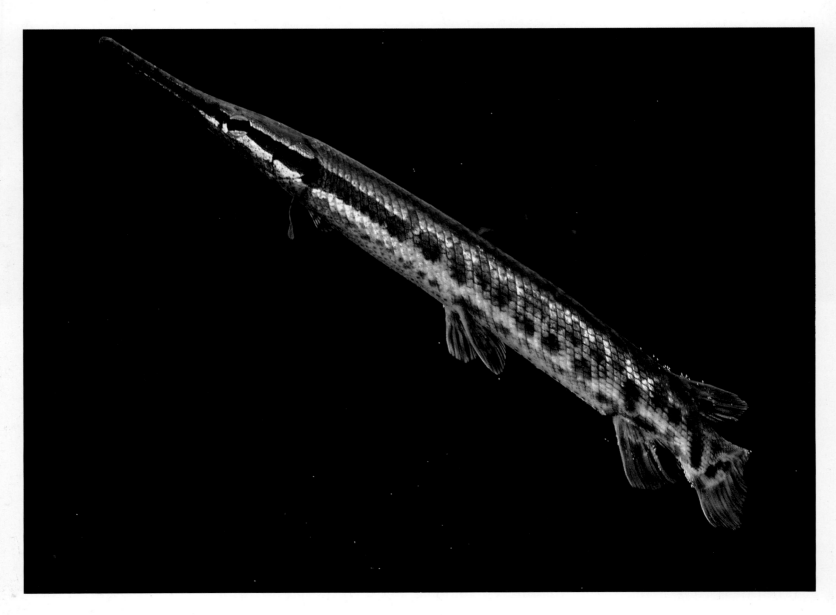

The body of the garpike, Lepisosteus osseus, is heavily armored with thick scales, giving it a very primitive appearance. Indeed, fossil evidence suggests that these fish have remained unchanged for approximately 65 million years.

With the skill and accuracy of a marksman, the archerfish, Toxotes jaculator, is able to spit a jet of water at insects resting on leaves on (or even flying over) any body of water where these hungry predators reside.

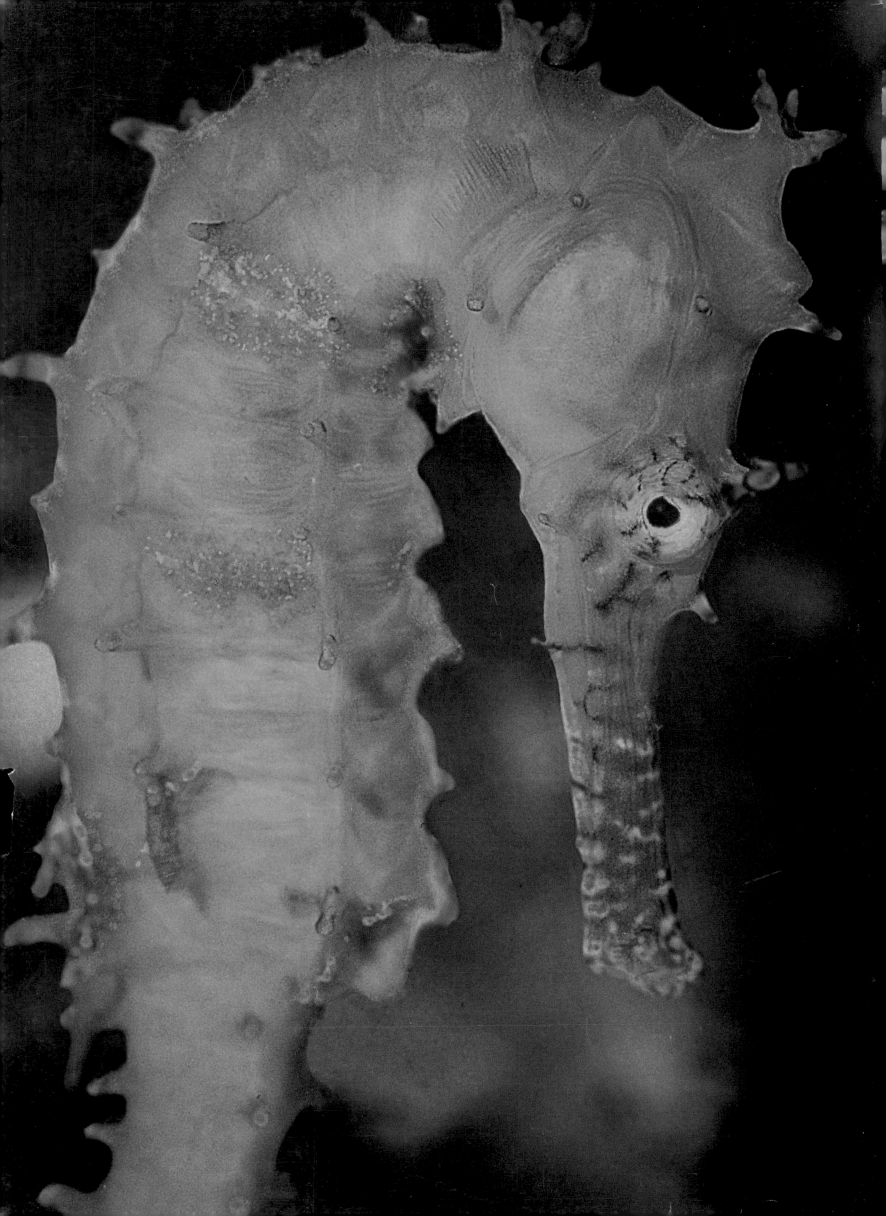

THE AQUARIUM: A WORLD IN MINIATURE

In their natural environment, most fish live in large bodies of water. Even a small pond is larger than the average home aquarium, so keeping fish in the artificial conditions of a small aquarium is likely to put them under stress unless the conditions are completely to their liking.

Setting Up An Aquarium

The first consideration should be the position of the aquarium. It should not be placed where it will get a lot of sun, because this can lead to overheating and a continuous, problematic growth of algae on the glass. In a shaded spot the lighting can be regulated and algal growth kept to a minimum. The tank should also be kept away from drafts, as these can cause temperature loss. Avoid, too, places where people may knock into the aquarium or where it becomes an obstruction.

A full aquarium is very heavy and needs a specially constructed stand. Even an average-size domestic aquarium weighs around 880 pounds (400 kilograms) when filled, so no

Despite their fragile appearance, seahorses, Hippocampus reidi, *make surprisingly hardy aquarium occupants when kept with similarly peaceful species. Under the right conditions, it is not unusual for them to breed in captivity.*

Only when this firefish, Nemateleotris splendida, *is confident it has a safe hole to retreat to, will it take on the flame-red coloration that gives the species its name. If a suitable site is not provided in the aquarium, this fish will busily set about making its own.*

*This half-masked cory, **Corydorus ambiacus**, is representative of a group of catfish that, without question, are the most popular kept in captivity. Their small size and peaceful nature make them the ideal occupants for the bottom layers of any community aquarium.*

ordinary shelf or piece of furniture is strong enough. (Be sure, too, that the floor beneath the stand is sturdy.) A stand which incorporates some storage space beneath it is very useful for housing pumps and filters, food, and cleaning equipment.

It also is important that the aquarium has its own electrical socket to supply the lighting, heater, and filters. These should not be unplugged at any time, so a socket which also has to supply other appliances may not be safe.

The aquarium should, if possible, be made entirely of glass; metal structures corrode easily in constant contact with water. A marine aquarium should have no metal parts

at all, as sea water is extremely corrosive. Choose equipment from a reliable dealer and follow his or her guidance as to how the tank should be set up.

Only purchase fish from a reputable dealer. It should be obvious by observing them in the dealer's tanks if the fish are alert and healthy. Ask to watch the fish feeding; if they show no interest in food they may not be healthy. And be sure that the aquarium is ready to receive fish and has been properly established before they are taken home; all lights, filters, and other equipment must be in working order before any fish are introduced.

18

In its natural environment this Moorish idol, Zanclus canescens, is a peaceable schooling fish of relatively open water. It requires a huge amount of swimming space; as a result, it often proves very temperamental and difficult to keep in the confines of an aquarium.

Some aquarists have a morbid fascination for venomous fish, but considering the lion fish's marvelous coloration and bold indifference to its surroundings, it is not difficult to see how the Pterios volitans has become so popular.

The Marine Aquarium

Keeping fish in a marine aquarium can be a very difficult task. Maintaining the correct salinity of the water is very tricky, and providing high enough oxygen levels in a well-stocked tank is also a challenge.

The great majority of marine fish kept in aquaria are tropical species which, in the wild, inhabit coral reefs. The reef provides very stable environmental conditions, so these fish are rather intolerant of fluctuations. On the reef, oxygen levels are always high and the light is very bright, as coral grows only in very shallow, clear water. Temperatures are constant and the water is kept in good condition, free from waste, by the constant flow of fresh seawater.

Seawater is highly corrosive, so the tank must be made entirely of glass or plastic, with no metal parts at all. (Metal not only corrodes badly, but also dissolves in the water, poisoning the fish, even in small quantities.) While marine fish are less inclined to jump out of the tank than freshwater fish, there is a risk that contaminants may drop in, so the tank must be covered very carefully. This will also help control evaporation; as water evaporates the salinity increases, so the tank must be topped off with distilled water.

Very bright lighting is also important in a marine aquarium. This encourages the growth of algae, which helps to remove some of the waste from the fish and is in turn eaten by the fish. Seawater is a complex mixture of salts at a concentration of approximately 3.5 parts per thousand. The largest constituent is sodium chloride, or common salt, but many other salts, in lesser amounts, are also present. It used to be very difficult to make artificial seawater because of the great number of trace elements present, but now excellent synthetic seawater can be made by mixing commercially prepared salts with tap water.

Seawater is alkaline, but in an aquarium there is a tendency for it to become slightly acidic due to the build up of organic waste and the higher levels of carbon dioxide. Nitrogen levels can also build up in the

This unusual looking elephant-nosed fish, Gnathonemus petersii, *from central Africa, is one of a huge variety of electric fishes. The small electrical field this fish produces around its body varies according to the fish's level of stress. Scientists are exploring the commercial value of this species as an indicator of pollution in freshwater rivers and lakes.*

closed conditions of an aquarium, so the water must be tested regularly and filtration needs to be very efficient. Biological filters, in which a colony of bacteria break down waste drawn into the gravel, are very effective, provided the current is strong enough to constantly draw waste down into the gravel. External filters are sometimes used in addition to biological filters; these help to maintain very clean conditions.

In the marine aquarium, a foamy scum usually builds up on top of the tank; this scum is like the albumen in eggs, removed by bacteria in the wild. A protein skimmer, powered by an air pump, can be used to remove this surface layer from the aquarium. Despite the difficulties of maintaining water quality, once a routine has been established to test the water regularly and scrupulously remove any dead or waste material, an established tank with the correct balance of fish and other creatures will remain trouble-free for very long periods.

If about one quarter of the water in the tank is changed every two months or so, being replaced with freshly made artificial sea water, the community can continue indefinitely.

Breeding Fish at Home

Breeding fish in captivity requires more skill on the part of the aquarist than does simply keeping them in good condition. Breeding is often stimulated in the wild by a change in the seasons, such as an increase in the length of daylight or a rise in water temperature in the spring. Fish also need to be in peak condition in order to breed successfully, therefore it is important for the aquarist to know a good deal about the life and habits of the fish in their natural habitat and to watch for the signs of readiness to breed among the captive fish. In the confines of an aquarium it is very likely that the eggs will be eaten, so it is preferable to provide a separate tank for spawning to allow them to hatch in safety.

The nocturnal habits and predatory behavior of the longjaw squirrelfish, Holocentrus marianus, do not make them the most popular of marine aquarium specimens. Nonetheless, their shoaling activity and red color can make a specialist tank containing six or more of the fish a truly spectacular sight.

The Arowana, **Osteoglossum bicirrhosum**, *can reach an awesome size; only very young specimens can be kept in aquaria. Take on the responsibility of these giants only if you can provide them with the space they require to grow.*

Pipefish, **Syngnathus grisseolineatus,** *make wonderful additions to small, calm aquariums. Provided there are lots of hiding places among algae and an almost constant supply of small, live food, they will continue to thrive for many years.*

FAMILIES OF FRESHWATER FISH

The Cyprinids are the familiar carp family, containing many common species of fresh-water river fish such as carp, bream, roach, and tench. Goldfish—the first true aquarium fish—are Cyprinids, but now about three hundred other species of Cyprinid are also kept by aquarists. In all there are about 1,500 species in this family, found around the world except in Australia and Antarctica. Most species come from rivers, so they are rather active in a still-water aquarium where there is no strong current to swim against. Many Cyprinids are shoaling fish and will not thrive if kept singly.

Cyprinids

There is a great range of sizes and shapes in this family, from tiny barbs at only 3/4 inch (2 centimeters) long, to the magnificent Indian mahseer at over 6 1/2 feet (2 meters) (although this is most certainly not an aquarium fish). The typical member of this family has an elongated body with large scales and a conventional arrangement of fins. The sexes normally look alike except when the females are ready to spawn and are full of roe, making them look more rounded. Cyprinids' mouths, which often have bar-bels at the sides, can be quite large, and some have a few blunt teeth in the throat to grind food.

Barbs are widespread warm-water Cyprinids found across Africa and Asia. They need high levels of oxygen and are lively swimmers. Many of them take well to life in an aquari-

The underslung mouth of the red-fin shark, **Labeo erythrurus**, *has lips that have evolved into sucking organs, within which are rows of horny teeth. Unlike the true shark, this small, freshwater fish feeds by using its specially adapted mouth to rasp algae off rocks.*

um and can usually be encouraged to breed under the right conditions. Rasboras are found in Malaysia and Indonesia; there are about thirty species. These are small, fast-swimming fish which live in shoals and prefer fast-flowing water. It is somewhat difficult to encourage rasboras to breed, as they require acidic water and readily eat their eggs as soon as they have been released.

Danios are Cyprinids found on the Indian subcontinent as well as in Sri Lanka and Burma. They are tolerant of a wider range of conditions and are relatively easy to breed. These are surface feeders and quite active in the aquarium.

Goldfish, Carassius auratus, *are incredibly tolerant of poor water quality, a trait which is often misinterpreted as meaning that these fish are easy to keep in aquariums. However, a large aquarium with consistent water conditions is essential for these fish to thrive in captivity.*

The brilliant metallic red of this male rosy barb, **Barbus conchonius,** *is only this intense when the fish is in breeding condition. Otherwise the species remains a less exciting, but nonetheless attractive, silvery color.*

The bizarre-looking pearl scale Carassius auratus, *is classified as exactly the same species as the common goldfish. Its appearance is a result of years of selective breeding to accentuate its interesting features.*

Fancy varieties of goldfish such as this red-cap oranda, Carassius auratus, *are often less tolerant of fluctuations in water conditions than the normal varieties and, as such, are not a good idea for anyone new to fish-keeping.*

Perfectly adapted to its life in the fast-flowing streams of Southeast Asia, the pearl danio, Brachydanio albolineatus, *also thrives in aquaria where this sort of swirling turbulence, recreated by modern power filters, is provided.*

Characins

Many very popular and well-known species of aquarium fish are Characins. It is a very large and diverse family, diplaying a wide range of adaptations to varied conditions in freshwater. Most are found in the rivers of Central and South America, especially the Amazon, but a few species live in North America and in northern Africa.

Size and body shape can vary widely; some Characins are flattened laterally for swimming between plant stems, while others are elongated and have round bodies designed for fast swimming against strong currents. Male Characins have a very tiny hook at the tip of the rays on the anal fin, and a few species have hooks on other fins as well; this is a useful guide to the sexes when attempting to breed Characins. If Characins are caught in a very fine mesh net small males may cling to the net momentarily.

Unlike the Cyprinids, Characins have teeth; the most striking example is the notorious piranha. Not all varieties have such large

teeth, however; many have smaller and more numerous teeth. Fish that have teeth are most likely to be carnivorous, feeding on organisms smaller than themselves. In the aquarium they appreciate live food such as daphnia or tubifex, but they can also live on high-quality dried foods.

Between the dorsal fin and the tail of Characins is a small, fleshy adipose fin which has no fin rays (this feature is also found in members of the salmon family). The function of this fin is not clear. There are a few Characins which do not conform to this standard pattern: They have lost the adipose fin as well as their teeth.

If an attempt is made to breed Characins, they must be given live food, but this is a very difficult group to raise in captivity. Commercial breeders raise Characins, but those reared from several generations in captivity are usually far less striking than their wild counterparts. There is less competition in the aquarium, so the need for bright coloration is reduced and the captive stock

With its large size and primarily vegetarian feeding habits, this banded leporinus, Leporinus fasciatus, will make short work of any soft, feathery leafed plants in the aquarium. Supplement the fish's diet with frozen spinach, and decorate its aquarium with only the hardiest of plants.

The striking black coloration of this delightful tetra is the only similarity the black widow, *Gymnocorymbus ternetzi*, has with its deadly arachnid namesake. Its peaceful, shoaling activity will liven up any well-planted community aquarium.

The bulging chest of the silver hatchetfish, *Gasteropelecus levis*, encloses muscles that power the long pectoral fins found in this family. These muscles are used for a powered "flight" across the surface of the water, enabling the fish to escape would-be predators.

Like many tetras, this cardinal tetra, Cheirodon axelrodi, is happiest in a shoal. Their vivid blue and red colors intensify if these fish are kept in a well-planted aquarium filled with soft water.

The red spot on the side of this bleeding-heart tetra, Hyphessobrycon erythrostigma, demonstrates how the fish got its name. Its subtle coloring can add a refreshing contrast to an aquarium containing a lively shoal of vividly colored tetras.

gradually becomes less attractive in appearance. Nonetheless, it is preferable to breed the fish in captivity rather than continually catching them in the wild. Not only is it bad conservation practice, but there is also a greater risk of introducing diseases when fish are taken from rivers.

The tetras are the most popular species in this large family. There are only two genera—*Hyphessobrycon* and *Hemigrammus*—which are true tetras, but, unfortunately, most other small Characins are given this name as well. Taxonomists have attempted to correct the nomenclature, but aquarists still call a wide variety of fish tetras.

Cyprinodonts

This family is also known as egg-laying toothcarps or killifish. They are widespread across most of the tropics, though they are not found in Australia or the East Indies. The natural habitat of most toothcarps is small pools with plenty of vegetation. The water is often very acidic as a result of the build-up of decaying plant material, so keeping these fish in an aquarium requires very special conditions. Although they may be compatible with other fish in terms of behavior, few other species can tolerate the acid water conditions, so toothcarps are usually kept in single-species tanks.

Most toothcarps have cylindrical bodies designed for fast swimming, with the dorsal and anal fins positioned far back. The tail is frequently deeply forked, a further adaptation to fast swimming. Most species have a large mouth, typical of predators, but they can usually be kept with other fish provided they are not much smaller than the toothcarps.

Toothcarps are usually small and elongated and best suited to surface feeding. Insects are frequently taken, but they also feed on small fish. Dried food is not very popular with

them in the aquarium, so frequent meals of live food are necessary.

Some toothcarps, such as the egg-buriers, have very strange life cycles. They live in temporary pools which are subject to rapid drying, so they must lay eggs which are resistant to drought. These fish rely on sudden rain storms to fill their pools, stimulate the eggs to hatch, and enable them to feed, grow, and complete their life cycle in a very short time before the pool dries up once more.

The live-bearing toothcarps give birth to live young; this is possible because the fertilized eggs are retained inside the female's body until they have hatched. These species are confined to the Americas, and live in freshwater, brackish water, and, very occasionally, the sea itself. The females are generally larger than the males, and when carrying developing eggs become very fat. Males have a specially adapted anal fin which allows them to deposit sperm inside the female; this usually follows a frenzied courtship display, with the tiny male doing his utmost to interest a normally disinterested female.

If mated in captivity the females must be left completely undisturbed, as they will readily abort their brood. Once fertilized, however, the female can produce several broods from one deposit of sperm. The brood is usually very small, and the tiny young are able to start feeding as soon as they are born. The live-bearing toothcarps are quite tolerant of a wide range of conditions in the aquarium, and, if kept in good condition, they will breed quite freely.

Cichlids

This important group of freshwater fish is found over a wide area, ranging from the southern United States and Central and South America to Africa, the Middle East, India, and Sri Lanka. Aquarists, however, are most interested in the species from Africa and the Americas.

The African cichlids are comparatively small and come from a variety of habitats. West African species usually live in acid waters where there is a lot of vegetation. East African species, most of which are found in Lake Malawi, come in a wonderful range of colors, many of them rivaling marine species. The size and varied conditions of the lake have given rise to an immense variety of

species, most of which are small and strongly territorial. They require hard, alkaline water with salt added to it. Several other East African lakes have populations of cichlids as well; since they normally inhabit these large lakes, they are rather slow moving in the aquarium.

The American cichlids are also very numerous and varied, although only the smaller species, commonly known as dwarf cichlids, are likely to be kept in the aquarium. These are suitable for community tanks, only becoming aggressive towards other fish when breeding.

Cichlids have many physical characteristics similar to their relative the common perch, particularly the large, spiny-rayed fins. Body shape can vary from streamlined and elongated to rounded, and sometimes flattened. All of the species have spiny fins and a lateral line divided into two parts.

Cichlids are best kept by specialists who are interested in them for their breeding behavior and color changes. These are predatory fish and have strong teeth, so they are usually kept in single-species aquaria. A few live in shoals, but when they reach breeding condition they become territorial and drive other fish away. Most have aggressive habits and will disturb the gravel, uprooting plants, so

The tapering snout of this butterfly fish, Pantodon buchholzi, disguises an otherwise enormous mouth that is ever ready to engulf anything that passes by. In the aquarium, these fish often prove difficult to feed, requiring a ready supply of suitably sized live food.

their tanks can not easily be kept in an attractive condition.

If cichlids are introduced to a tank as immature fish they will not be aggressive toward each other, but if two adults are introduced they will fight furiously. Separating them by a sheet of glass until they become tolerant of each other often works. Adults can be brought to breeding condition by giving them plenty of live food and keeping the temperature of the tank a little warmer than normal. They can be encouraged to breed by placing them in a large tank without plants but with a good selection of rocks, upturned flowerpots, or driftwood. Many breed in caves, so if the materials in the tank are

Following page: Named after a famous boxer, the Jack Dempsey, Cichlasoma octofasciatum, deserves its name. In the aquarium, it is incredibly pugnacious and should not be kept with any other fish.

In the calcium-rich waters of Lake Tanganyika, these Brichards' cichlids, Lamprologus brichardi, form part of a massive community of similar fish species holding territories among the boulders. Although unsuitable for a normal aquarium, Brichards' cichlid makes a peaceful addition to a community of related species.

This zebra angelfish's (Pterophyllum scalare) laterally compressed shape and vertical stripes are perfect adaptations to living in the weedy, slow-moving rivers of South America, where it is able to hide among tree roots and prey on invertebrates and small fish.

The discus, Symphysodon aequifasciata, is a very delicate fish that does not adjust instantly to aquarium conditions. It is often viewed as the ultimate challenge to many freshwater fish-keepers.

arranged in such a way as to form good hiding places these will be readily used.

If conditions meet with their approval a pair of adults will choose a nesting site and carefully clean it of all debris. The sticky eggs are guarded until they have hatched, and the young are watched very carefully as they take their first few meals. As long as the adults are not disturbed they will look after the young quite well, but it may be necessary to remove some of them to a separate tank if there are

signs of their being eaten. The fry need to be raised on a diet of live food such as brine shrimp and daphnia. Adults are eager feeders, taking not only live food, including large items like earthworms, but also dried food and some plant material.

Anabantidae

This group is more commonly known as labyrinth fish because of a special organ they possess which enables them to breathe air from the surface. As a result of this ability they are very adaptable, and can live in conditions which would kill other fish. Siamese fighting fish are a very well known species of labyrinth fish, as are gouramis and climbing perches.

The labyrinth organ is made up of a series of bony plates covered with thin tissues set inside cavities on either side of the head. This creates a large surface area through which oxygen can be absorbed. Some labyrinth fish are so dependent on this method of breathing that they will die if they are not able to reach the surface and take in air; they make regular trips to the surface, normally about three times a

Many cichlids show a degree of parental care which sets them apart from many other fish species. This brightly colored Lake Nyasa cichlid, Pseudotropheus elongatus, takes parenthood so seriously that it broods its newly hatched young in its mouth.

The spectacular colors and long fins of the Siamese fighting fish, Betta splendens, are instantly recognizable to both hobbyists and other male fighting fish. If two males are placed together, these fish will instantly set about proving how they got their name.

Like many of the fish that give birth to live young, the swordtail, Xiphophorus helleri, is easy to breed in captivity. Unfortunately, its readiness to breed with the closely related platies, Xiphophorus maculatus, has resulted in a mish-mash of non-specific variations being available in the trade.

Although incredibly popular with many newcomers to fish-keeping, the black mollie, Poecilia latipinna, is not the easiest of fish to keep healthy in the aquarium. It does best in a tank to which a small amount of sea salt has been added.

The blue gourami, Trichogaster trichopterus, is one of many variations of this species available in the aquarium trade. Looking at this specimen, it is difficult to see how this fish got its other common name, three-spot gourami.

The small size, bright colors, and tolerance of a variety of condi tions have made the fancy guppy, Poecilia reticulata, a favorite with hobbyists for decades. An easy fish to breed in captivity, this species has been selectively bred to produce varia tions in tail size, shape, and color.

The dwarf gourami, Colisia lalia, is an incredibly hardy little fish and will readily breed in captivity. The male constructs a floating bubble nest out of saliva and pieces of plant debris, and guards it against any potential threat.

minute, in order to release a bubble of used air and take in a fresh supply. Newly hatched fish breathe in the normal way, through their gills, but after a few weeks, when they increase in size, they need to supplement their oxygen intake with the aid of the labyrinth.

Labyrinth fish have remarkably flexible bodies, with all the internal organs compressed into a small space near the head. Most are aggressive, especially when breeding, and are best kept away from other species.

This group has a unique method of caring for their eggs: The male produces a raft of bubbles, releasing mucus from his mouth to bind them together. Sometimes pieces of floating plant material are incorporated into the bubble nest to help strengthen it.

Males have a very elaborate courtship display and can become quite aggressive toward females if they do not respond favorably. A non-responsive female may not be ready to

In the wild the brilliant colors of the male guppy, Poecilia retiiculata, *are aimed at enticing the females to breed. In adopting this strategy, the male guppy makes himself far more obvious to predators than the well-camouflaged female.*

The beautifully marked pearl gourami, Trichogaster leeri, *is slightly more delicate than its hardy relatives. Its trailing, filamentous fins can encourage antisocial fin nipping in otherwise peaceful community fish such as barbs.*

The unusual, transparent body of the glass catfish, Krypopterus bicir-rhus, with its visible internal organs and skeleton, makes this fish very popular as a novelty.

Many killifish, such as this lace-finned species, Pterolebias zonatus, have a very short life cycle and, once they have spawned, they will often die. This curious situation is an extraordinary adaptation to living in the shallow pools of the tropics, which dry up with the change of seasons.

spawn, so she needs somewhere to hide from the male, preferably among thickly planted vegetation. If the female is receptive she will remain near the male's bubble nest, and he will turn her upside down by wrapping himself around her. Once the eggs are released, the male fertilizes them, draws them into his mouth, and then squirts them into the nest; in some species the female helps him do this. The male may try to mate with the female again if all of her eggs were not released the first time, but once the pair is done the male drives the female away.

After mating, the male remains on guard, retrieving any eggs that fall out of the nest and jetting them back into the bubbles with his mouth. He also watches out for any young which escape from the nest and ensures that they are safely returned. The newly hatched young are very difficult to rear, requiring minute live food and warm water, but once they have matured they are very hardy.

Catfish

Catfish are characterized by having sensory barbels around the mouth which enable them to find food on the bottom of muddy rivers and lakes. There are about two thousand species of catfish, all of which are very varied. They can be found in a number of different types of habitat, from clear, fast-flowing mountain streams to slow-moving and sometimes stagnant waters. Many are resis-

The long barbels around the mouth of this polka-dot, or pim pictus, cat-fish, **Pimelodus pictus,** *have very sensitive taste cells at their tips, enabling the fish to find food in the murkiest of waters, even at night.*

tant to unpleasant conditions which would kill other fish.

Some catfish have sucker-like mouths which enable them to browse on algae or cling to stones in very fast currents. A few species are aggressive and predatory, but most are quiet scavengers who stay near the bottom searching for food. Some are nocturnal feeders, remaining hidden during the day.

The legendary red-tailed catfish, **Phractocephalus hemioliopterus,** *has the potential to reach an enormous size in the aquarium, and will eat anything it can fit into its mouth. They are only suitable for enthusiasts who can accommodate these greedy monsters.*

Cobitidae

The Cobitidae, or loaches, are quite widespread; they can be found across Europe and throughout Asia and North Africa. They bear a superficial resemblance to the catfish, having barbels around the mouth. In the wild loaches prefer fast-flowing rivers, and spend most of their time sheltering among stones waiting for food to be swept towards them. They have no visible scales on the body, which is usually elongated and eel-like.

Loaches require high levels of oxygen; some supplement what they obtain through their gills by gulping down a mouthful of air from the surface from time to time. Waste gases leave the body through the vent. Loaches can detect changes in atmospheric pressure, and become restless when the weather is about to change; one species, known as the weatherfish, has been kept as a form of living barometer for centuries.

Most loaches appreciate a diet of live food, although they are unable to catch fast-moving prey. They are good burrowers, constantly snuffling through the gravel in search of a meal.

Often seen as juveniles in aquarium stores, the somewhat temperamental clown loach, **Botia macracantha,** *has the potential to reach a surprisingly large size in captivity; in very large aquaria these attractive fish can reach 12 inches (30 centimeters) in length.*

It is said that the weather loach, **Misgurnus anguilicaudatus,** *is sensitive to changes in barometric pressure and can predict the coming of a storm with frantic swimming, a marked change from this fish's normally peaceful behavior.*

FAMILIES OF MARINE FISH

A great number of families of marine fish are found in the world's seas and oceans, but only a few of them are suitable for keeping in an aquarium. Many live only in the deepest oceans or grow to an immense size, while others are such specialized feeders that it is impossible to keep them healthy in captivity. Only those families which are easily obtained and thrive in captivity are described here.

Chaetodontidae

The Chaetondontidae, or butterfly fish, are attractive, reef-dwelling fish of tropical seas. They typically have flattened bodies and spiny dorsal fins. Their mouths are usually tiny and beak-like so they can pick out morsels of food from crevices in the reef. A number of species are very specialized feeders, living in association with a particular species of coral, and are not easy to keep in

The false eye spots on the flanks of the four-eye butterfly fish, Chaetodon capistratus, *act as a decoy to confuse potential predators. As a result of this bit of visual deception, the fish is able to flee from an attack in the opposite direction to that anticipated by its predator.*

This ornate coralfish, Chaetodon ornatissimus, inhabits the outer reefs of Hawaii and the western Pacific where it swims freely with its own and other, closely related species. In the aquarium, however, this species can be pugnacious and completely intolerant of other fish.

With its upper and lower jaws extended into a needle-sharp point, this brilliantly colored long-nosed butterfly fish, Forcipiger flavissimus, certainly has an advantage when it comes to picking tiny morsels of food from between coral heads on the reefs where it resides.

The submissive, head-down posture of this raccoon butterfly fish, Chaetodon iunuia, is part of a ritualistic display performed by all fish when receiving the services of the cleaner-wrasse.

the aquarium. Most, however, are fairly tolerant of other fish and can live in a well-heated aquarium with high salinity. So far, butterfly fish have not been bred in captivity, but when given a good, varied diet with plenty of live food they can be kept in healthy condition.

Labridae

The wrasse family is a large and widespread group comprising about six hundred species, several of which live in the cold waters around the shores of northwestern Europe. They are strong swimmers with elongated, muscular bodies; they propel themselves forwards with powerful movements of their pectoral fins, and can dive down to the bottom to dig into gravel quite easily. Some small species will actually bury themselves in the sand at night, and many will hide in the gravel when first introduced to a new tank.

Aquarists not familiar with the habits of the wrasse may be surprised to see a large fish lying on its side on the bottom of the tank in a deep sleep. A coating of mucus is sometimes secreted to cover and protect the body at night.

All of the species have strong teeth and jaws which they use to crush the shells of mollusks and crustaceans. They eat a variety of foods, but prefer that which they can literally sink their teeth into. Once they have settled into an aquarium wrasse become relatively bold and can be fed easily, but they require special care for the first few days.

In the wild, it is not uncommon for wrasse such as this harlequin wrasse, **Lienardella fasciata,** *to change their sex. Normally the dominant females of a single-sex group undergo this role reversal and, invariably, the largest, most colorful fish are males.*

Four-spot butterfly fish, **Chaetodon quadrimaculatus,** *are relatively small and may lack confidence in an aquarium containing larger, more boisterous fish. As a result, they tend to spend much of their time hiding and miss out in the rush for food.*

Despite being almost exclusively carnivorous, these rainbow wrasse, Cheillinus undulatus, *are surprisingly tolerant of other fish species. Their elongated bodies and dazzling colors make them an interesting addition to any marine community.*

The coloration of this huge, adult Spanish hogfish, Bodianus rufus, bears little resemblance to the smaller blue and yellow specimens often seen in aquarium shops. Like many wrasse, the juveniles of this species will often perform cleaning services for other fish in the aquarium.

Pomacentridae

This family includes the damselfish and the clownfish, both very popular with marine aquarists. They are very hardy in the aquarium and seem to be tolerant of a range of conditions. Most are very easy to feed, taking a wide range of foods, and do not grow to a great size, so several can be kept in a moderate-size tank. They are more tolerant than most reef fish of a build-up of nitrites in the water, so they are sometimes used to help prepare a tank for other more sensitive inhabitants: The nitrogenous waste they release helps to build a bacterial colony in the gravel; these bacteria will later process the nitrites released into the water.

One of the interesting features of damselfish is their highly territorial behavior. In a large enough tank with a varied arrangement of rocks and coral this should be no problem, but if new fish are introduced to a small tank with an established population of damselfish there will be some very serious territorial disputes, and smaller fish may suffer injuries.

Damselfish can be bred in the aquarium given good conditions, but the tiny young are difficult to feed unless a supply of a minute form of live food is available.

Clownfish are brightly colored, rounded

fish like the damsels, but they have the habit of living in a partnership with large sea anemones. Although anemones feed on small fish and invertebrates, clownfish are able to protect themselves by covering their bodies with a mixture of their own mucus and that produced by the anemone; the anemone is then unable to recognize the fish as prey. Some clownfish can live away from anemones, but a few species do not thrive unless they are in partnership. They lay their eggs at the base of their anemone host, and these hatch freely, but the minute young will

This delightful little fish is commonly called the humbug due to its similarity in color to a popular confection. The colors of the black-and-white damselfish, **Dascyllus aruanus**, *can create an interesting contrast against the vivid colors of a mature marine aquarium.*

Anemone fish such as these orange-fin **Amphiprion chrysopterus** *are able to live within the stinging tentacles of the anemone without injury, thanks to a protective layer of mucus on the fish's body. In the aquarium, these fish will readily form a close relationship with any suitable anemone.*

Damselfish such as this golden damselfish, **Amblyglyphidoden aureus**, *make ideal first fish for those just starting a marine aquarium. They are energetic, adapt well to life in captivity, and are tolerant of the fluctuations in water quality that can occur when setting up smaller aquaria.*

The emperor angelfish, Pomacanthus imperator, is frequently encountered in the aquarium trade and has become a favorite with marine fish keepers but, like all angels, this species is very sensitive to poor water quality.

feed only on microscopic plankton. This can only be provided by supplying fresh seawater very regularly. In fact, clownfish are generally less tolerant of poor water quality than damselfish, and are most content when there are frequent water changes.

The anemone hosts can be kept healthy by giving them small pieces of chopped fish. They also require very bright lighting, because they have symbiotic algae living inside them which require light to photosynthesize. Anemones, too, are happiest if the water is changed frequently.

Serranidae

This family is more familiarly known as groupers, large fish found in tropical and temperate waters. Some reach enormous sizes and can be quite tame when encountered by divers. Their bodies are solid and powerful,

with spiny fins and attractive markings. Only a few species are small enough to be kept in aquaria. They are usually very secretive, remaining hidden for long periods and only emerging when food is offered, quickly returning to their hiding places when the meal is over. Groupers can wedge themselves into crevices in coral if alarmed, but normally they just hover or swim very slowly around a small area.

Groupers' mouths are very large and have an extendible lower jaw, so they can eat pieces of fish or meat. In a community tank they will not bother other fish that are too large to gulp down, but they should not be kept with very small species.

Unfortunately, groupers are too large when mature to breed successfully in an aquarium. It is interesting, though, to speculate how they were named groupers, as one thing they can not do successfully is live together in a group.

Pomacanthinae

The Pomacanthinae—angelfish—are similar to butterfly fish (to which they are related), but they have thicker bodies and a sharp spine on the lower edge of the gill covers. They can become quite large and are

The spectacular colors on this regal angelfish, **Pygoplites diacanthus,** *make it easy to see how it got its name. It is, however, a shy species that is difficult to acclimatize to aquarium conditions.*

*Although a very attractive species, the rock beauty, Holacanthus
tricolor, is a very large fish which requires a spacious aquarium.
In its native habitat on the reefs of the western Atlantic, this fish
eats sponges, so it is difficult to feed under aquarium conditions.*

The colors of this adult French angel, Pomacanthus paru, *are quite different from the vivid black and yellow stripes seen on the juveniles of this species. Here the spine on the gill cover, which distinguishes angelfish from the similar butterfly fish, is clearly visible.*

beautifully colored. Angelfish are highly territorial and fight others of their own species quite aggressively, but they are usually less combative when given a cave in the coral in which to hide from time to time.

At one time the young and adults were thought to be separate species because of their completely different markings and colors. It was only through observing them in aquaria that the color changes were discovered and the relationship between these seemingly different fish realized.

This family has very exacting requirements for food, which must contain some vegetable matter, and water conditions, which must remain constant.

Acanthuridae

This family includes the surgeonfish, or tangs, which are noted for having a large, erect spine on either side of the tail. This spine is used in self-defense, and can inflict a nasty wound on the hand of an aquarist who does not use a net when handling one of these fish.

Tangs have rather thickened, oval-shaped bodies and are brightly colored. In the wild, they live in shoals, but they are unable to tolerate their own kind in an aquarium. They must be given some vegetable food in order to keep them healthy, but even with the best of diets, tangs do not to settle enough to breed in captivity.

Following page: A real supermodel of the fish world, this aptly named lipstick tang, Naso lituratus, has spectacularly well defined facial markings said to resemble makeup. These colors contrast greatly with the pale gray that covers much of the fish's body.

It is unusual to find a marine fish of only one color, but what this yellow tang, Zebrasoma flavescens, lacks in variety it certainly makes up for in sheer brilliance. A spacious aquarium containing a large shoal of these fish can create a stunning display.

An instantly recognizable sight to any hobbyist, the powder blue tang, Acanthurus leucosternon, is a common feature in most aquarium stores. Its bright colors and bold behavior make it one of the most popular marine fish kept in aquaria.

Surgeons such as this orangeband surgeon-fish, Acanthurus olivaceous, are so called because of the scalpel-like spine position-ed near the tail, used for defense and during territorial disputes with other fish.

Picasso triggerfish, Rhinecanthus aculeatus, are excessively aggressive towards other aquarium residents and should be kept on their own. Despite this, their greedy feeding habits, which make them ever ready to take food from the hands of their owners, make them very popular among marine aquarists.

The extraordinarily psychedelic markings of the clown triggerfish, Balistoides conspicillum, *actually act as camouflage against the coral-encrusted reefs of the Indo-Pacific where this fish is normally found. In the aquarium, however, its markings make it unmistakable.*

Balistidae

Balistidae, or triggerfish, are noted for having huge heads which sometimes comprise one-third of the body length. The dorsal fin has a huge spine which can be raised and jammed against the roof of a cave to prevent the fish being pulled out by a predator. Their mouths are relatively small, but they have strong teeth and powerful jaws; they can easily nip fins, or even fingers, so they are best kept in tanks on their own. They should also be kept away from filter pipes and heater cables, as they will also nibble at these out of curiosity.

Triggerfish enjoy moving chunks of rock and coral around the tank, and, in the process, any invertebrates they find will be eaten. Because they are totally carnivorous, they need a diet of live shrimp and other hard-shelled foods.

Like the wrasse, triggerfish occasionally lie on their sides on the floor of the aquarium. In a large enough tank they will thrive and display other interesting behavior, including their strange method of swimming with undulating dorsal and anal fins and rigid bodies.

As with all triggerfish, the vivid patterns on this queen triggerfish, Balistes vetula, all seem to emphasize the mouth and head, which appear disproportionately large by comparison to the rest of the body. These markings advertise to potential predators that this fish is armed with a powerful set of teeth and jaws.

Ostraciontidae

This family is better known as the boxfish or cowfish; they have bodies encased in a rigid, box-like skin, with the eyes, mouth, and fins emerging through openings. They are curious, rather than attractive, because of their strange shape and awkward method of swimming, and are best kept alone because other fish tend to worry them. If threatened they release an unpleasant poison into the water which kills everything in the tank, including the boxfish.

Pufferfish and porcupine fish, which can inflate their bodies and erect spines for protection, are closely related species which can also be kept in a large tank.

*This curiously shaped long-horned cowfish, **Lactoria cornuta**, is able to buzz around with the precision of a helicopter. The propelling force is created by coordinated undulations of both the pectoral and dorsal fins.*

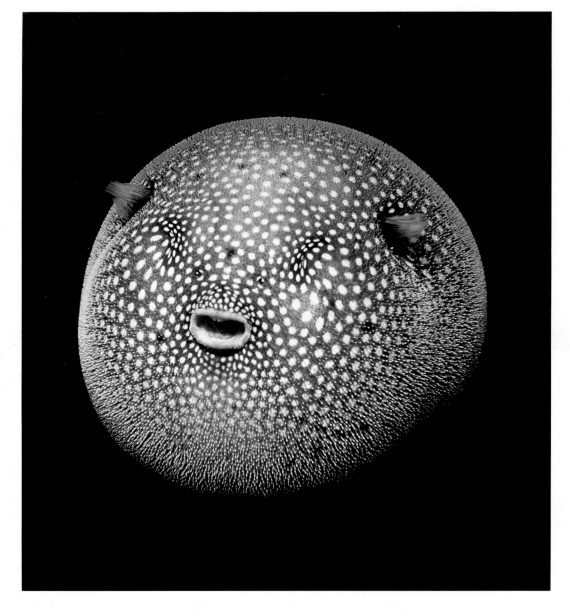

Inflating itself to bizarre proportions so that the spines on its body stand outward is this slow-moving spotted pufferfish's (Arothrodon meleagris) only means of defense. It is, however, unfair to encourage this fright response in captive animals.

*The orbiculate batfish, **Platax orbicularis**, can reach an enormous size in the wild. In captivity this species requires a deep aquarium, but is otherwise not fussy about its diet and minor fluctuations in salinity.*

INDEX

*Page numbers in **bold-face** type indicate photo captions.*